I0155498

RETHINKING THE LAW

ERIC LANE

Other books by Eric Lane

Eve's Story

I Want to be a Church Member

I Want to be Baptised

Psalms (2 Volumes)

Proverbs, Everyday Wisdom for Everyone

Special Children?

RETHINKING THE LAW

ERIC LANE

NEWCOVENANT
MEDIA

5317 Wye Creek Drive, Frederick, MD 21703-6938
301-473-8781 | info@newcovenantmedia.com
www.NewCovenantMedia.com

RETHINKING THE LAW

Copyright 2014 © by: Eric Lane

Published by: New Covenant Media
                  5317 Wye Creek Drive
                  Frederick, MD 21703-5938

Cover design by: Laura Bonser

Orders: www.newcovenantmedia.com

All rights reserved. No part of this publication may be reproduced, stored in a retrieval system, or transmitted in any form by any means, electronic, mechanical, photocopy, recording, or otherwise without the prior permission of the publisher, except as provided by USA copyright law.

Printed in the United States of America.

ISBN 13: 978-1-928965-62-6

Unless otherwise noted, all Scripture quotations are taken from THE HOLY BIBLE, NEW INTERNATIONAL VERSION®, NIV® Copyright © 1973, 1978, 1984, by Biblica, Inc.® Used by permission. All rights reserved worldwide.

Scripture quotations marked ESV are from The Holy Bible, English Standard Version® (ESV®), Copyright © 2001 by Crossway, a publishing ministry of Good News Publishers. Used by permission. All rights reserved.

Scripture quotations marked KJV are from The King James Version, commonly known as the Authorized Version or King James Bible.

Dedication

This book is dedicated to:

The members of Yateley Baptist Church,
who have prayed with me
in the production of this book.

Table of Contents

INTRODUCTION   1

CHAPTER 1 THE MEANING OF *LAW* IN SCRIPTURE   3

CHAPTER 2 LAW BEFORE THE LAW   17

CHAPTER 3 THE LAW OF MOSES   27

CHAPTER 4 THE TEN COMMANDMENTS   47

CHAPTER 5 THE PURPOSE OF THE LAW   69

CHAPTER 6 THE LAW IN THE TEACHING OF CHRIST   99

CHAPTER 7 LAW AND GOSPEL   113

CHAPTER 8 LAW AND LIBERTY   131

CHAPTER 9 SABBATH, LORD'S DAY OR SUNDAY?   149

CHAPTER 10 THE LAW AND HOLINESS   175

CONCLUSION   195

APPENDIX ON MATTHEW 5:17–20   201

SCRIPTURE INDEX   209

INDEX OF AUTHORS   223

BIBLIOGRAPHY   225

INTRODUCTION

The thesis of this book is that the Mosaic Law, the Law of Sinai, was a covenant between God and Israel, which is a foreshadowing of the new covenant between Christ and his church. This new covenant was in view from the time of Abraham and is clarified in the gospel, for the faith which justified Abraham (Gen. 15:6) is the faith in Christ by which we die to sin and rise to righteousness (Rom. 4:23–24, Gal. 3:6–9), a righteousness superior to that attainable under the Law (Matt. 5:20).

Indeed, rather than making sinners righteous, the Law exposed sin and condemned it (Rom. 7:10–13). But where the Law failed faith succeeds, not by slavish obedience to rules, but by union with Christ through the Spirit (Rom. 8:3–4). The obedience to which a Christian is called is an obedience which consists in bringing forth the fruit of the Spirit (Gal. 5:16–23). This truly fulfils the Law and safeguards against legalism. The position taken in this book is broadly that of *From Sabbath to Lord's Day*,[1] edited by D.A. Carson and the following quotation from the book is a good summary of the view of this present volume.

> The law presents mankind with the ethical standards of the holy God. As such, its goodness is unquestionable, but its effect is simply to demonstrate the existence of our sin, to condemn us as a result, and also to provoke our sin. Because of the weakness of the flesh, it can have no other effect on us when we read its righteous demands. Only death with Christ will remove us from the condemnation that it would otherwise

---

[1] D.A. Carson, ed., *From Sabbath to Lord's Day: A Biblical, Historical and Theological Investigation* (Eugene, OR: Wipf and Stock, 1999).

certainly pronounce on anyone who endeavoured to live by its standards.

But the law also stands for the whole covenantal arrangement that God made with His people at Sinai, a covenant that has now manifestly been replaced by the new covenant in Christ. In both of these aspects Paul realized that the law no longer played any role in the life of a Christian. His new and Christian insights into the "exceeding sinfulness of sin" also led him to see that any attempt, even by Christians, to use the law as a basis for standing before God led inevitably to the sin of boasting, that is, faith in self rather than faith in God. The only Christian way to fulfill one's obligations to God is by fulfilling the law of love (the law of subordinating oneself to the other), by walking in the Spirit. These two factors, love and the Spirit, Paul sees as keeping Christian obedience from degenerating into legalism. Too rarely, alas, has the church been able to preserve this Pauline insight.[2]

---

[2] D.R. de Lacey, "The Sabbath/Sunday Question and the Law in the Pauline Corpus" in *From Sabbath to Lord's Day,* ed., D.A. Carson (Eugene, OR: Wipf and Stock, 1999) 175.

CHAPTER 1
THE MEANING OF *LAW* IN SCRIPTURE

It is difficult to find a treatment of the subject of law in Scripture which begins by distinguishing the various meanings of the term *law* as used in the Bible. Most assume it always means the list of laws revealed by God to Moses at Sinai, especially the Ten Commandments. The Jews call this the *TORAH* and claim it is "five-fifths of the Law." It would seem that most writers on the subject of Law share this belief. But *law—NOMOS* in the Greek New Testament—has several distinct meanings. E.F. Kevan says this explains why Paul "argues against the Law in one sense and pleads for it in another."[3]

   1.   *In Romans 3:27 it has the meaning of **principle**:*
(A *principle* is a general rule or basic truth which can be applied to other matters).

>   *Where is boasting then? It is excluded. On what principle (NOMOS)? On that of works? No, but on the principle (NOMOS) of faith.*

The NIV translates *NOMOS, principle*, whereas the AV translates it *law*, as it does elsewhere. But the NIV rather muddies the waters by translating *works (ERGON)* as "observing the law," although the term *law (NOMOS)* is not in that part of the sentence. However, *principle* best fits Paul's argument here. In view of what he has just said about justification before God as being by faith (Rom. 3:26), he asks

---

[3] E.F. Kevan, *The Moral Law* (Jenkintown, PA: Sovereign Grace Publishers, 1963) 6.

where this leaves *boasting*, and replies "it is excluded." He then asks, "Through what *NOMOS*? Of works?" and answers "No, but through the *NOMOS* of faith." While it might be right to speak of the Sinai code as "a law of works," it is scarcely possible to speak of it as "a law of faith," since in Paul's teaching law and faith are opposites. Speaking of the fruit of the Spirit he writes:

against such things there is no law (Gal. 5:23b),

and in Galatians 3:12 he says

the law is not based on faith.

But faith *can* be spoken of as *a principle*, a principle which excludes boasting. Since faith is simply trust in the work of Christ, described in Romans 3:25, there is nothing left for a person to boast about, as he goes on to say in Romans 4:1–5. The same applies to Romans 7:21: "so I find this law at work: when I want to do good evil is right there with me" (cf. Rom. 7:23). He can scarcely mean the moral law here, since to have evil present with him is not exactly moral! Nor can it mean the Mosaic Law since nothing of that name appears in the writings of Moses. With this John Owen agrees:

An inward principle that moves and inclines constantly unto any action is called a law.[4]

This is also the case in Romans 8:2–4. *Law* in verse 2 is different from *law* in verses 3–4, where it refers to the Mosaic law. But in verse 2 it clearly has the sense of *principle*: "the law of the Spirit of life" and "the law of sin and death" are clearly principles.

If *NOMOS* here means *principle* in relation to faith, it must also mean principle in relation to works. This is the broadest use of the term. It is used thus in secular language for a

---

[4] John Owen, *Overcoming Sin and Temptation* (Wheaton, Illinois: Crossway, 2006) 234.

principle which regulates conduct: for example, laws of light, sound, growth, etc.

2. *It can mean the **Old Testament Scriptures**.*

The Jews divided their Scriptures into: **Law** or *TORAH* (the five books of Moses); **Prophets** or *NEBIM,* consisting of the Former Prophets (Joshua, Judges, Samuel and Kings) and the Latter Prophets (Isaiah, Jeremiah, Ezekiel and 'the Book of the Twelve'); and **Writings** or *KETUBIM* (Psalms, Proverbs, Job, Song, Ruth, Lamentations, Ecclesiastes and Esther, Daniel, Ezra–Nehemiah and Chronicles). Jesus referred to these in Luke 24:44 when he declared:

> *This is what I told you when I was still with you. Everything must be fulfilled that is written about me in the Law of Moses, the Prophets and the Psalms.*

(He used *psalms* rather than *writings* because it was normal to call a whole section after the name of the first book in it). This was just after he had spent the long walk from Jerusalem to Emmaus bringing out of "Moses and the Prophets those things concerning himself." Here, *Moses* is short for "the Law of Moses" and "the Writings" are not specified. He used the same formula in Matthew 5:17:

> *Do not think that I have come to abolish the Law or the Prophets; I have not come to abolish them but to fulfill them.*

In Matthew 5:18 he further abbreviates the expression and just mentions "the Law," but is clearly referring to all three sections of the Scriptures. In Matthew 5:20 he refers to "the teachers of the Law," meaning of the Scriptures generally. In Romans 3:19 Paul speaks of "what the Law says," but is referring to quotations he has just made from the Psalms. Since the Psalms are not in the books of Moses and therefore strictly speaking not part of the Law, he is clearly referring to the Scriptures as a whole. He is using the term in the same way as Jesus did. When Jesus quoted Psalm 82:6 in John

10:34 he described the saying as "your law." So the term *law* can refer to the Old Testament Scriptures. It is the equivalent, therefore, of the Word of God.

3.   *The most frequent use of the term law in Scripture is to describe the code of rules given to Israel by God at Sinai.*

John uses it in this sense in John 1:17:

> *For the Law was given through Moses, but grace and truth came by Jesus Christ.*

In Matthew 11:13 Christ said:

> *For all the Prophets and the Law prophesied until John* [the Baptist].

Paul frequently used the phrase "under the Law" to refer to those to whom the Sinai code was first given, the people of Israel. It is used in this sense in Romans 3:19:

> *Now we know that whatever the Law says it says to those who are under the law,*

that is, the people of Israel, who pledged themselves to it at Sinai (Ex. 19:8). It was this that distinguished Israel from the Gentiles who were "not under the Law." He makes this distinction in Romans 2:12–15, where he writes of "those who sin apart from the Law" compared to "those who sin under the Law." In Romans 2:14 he makes it clear that he is referring to "the Gentiles who do not have the Law," that is, are ignorant of the code of rules God revealed at Sinai.

The term can also be used of a single specific command in the code, such as "the law of the burnt offering" (Lev. 7:37 ESV). In the plural—*laws*—it means a number of these specific laws. But the singular "the law of Moses" can also refer to the whole collection. Deuteronomy 4:44 says:

> *This is the law Moses set before the Israelites*

which clearly refers to the whole code. 1 Kings 2:3 is the same:

> *Walk in his ways, and keep his decrees and commands, as written in the law of Moses.*

But since this code consists of many rules, Deuteronomy 4:45 adds:

> *these are the stipulations, decrees and **laws**.*

Laws, therefore, is virtually identical with commandments, ordinances, statutes and decrees, terms used frequently in Psalm 119. Paul uses it in the same way in Ephesians 2:15: "the law with its commandments and regulations."

4. *The Hebrew word for* Law—*TORAH*—*can mean simply* ***teaching***, although it normally refers to the Sinai code of laws. It comes from *HORAH*, meaning *to point out*, and it stands in the Bible *for authoritative direction*. It is repeatedly remarked by writers on the law of God that *"TORAH* is not to be identified with commanding law, but that it stands for the covenant instructions given by God to his people."[5] The teaching can be general and not necessarily ethical. For example, in Isaiah 1:10 the prophet says:

> *Hear the word of the Lord, you rulers of Sodom, listen to the law of our God, you people of Gomorrah.*

Since this is Hebrew poetry, the second line is exactly parallel to the first, so that by "the law of our God" Isaiah means the same as "the word of the Lord," the whole teaching of God, not just the Mosaic law. The same applies to Isaiah 51:4:

> *Listen to me, my people, hear me, my nation: the law will go out from me*

In Isaiah 42:4 in his prediction of the Messiah he says:

> *in his law the islands will put their hope,*

---

[5] E.F. Kevan, *Keep His Commandments* (London: Tyndale, 1964) 13.

meaning the Messiah's teaching rather than the laws of
Moses. The teaching of the Messiah, Jesus Christ, greatly
enlarged on the laws given to Moses, as can be seen in the
Sermon on the Mount.

The same applies in Proverbs 1:8:

> *Listen, my son, to your father's instruction and do not forsake
> your mother's teaching.*

The "father's instruction" is identical to the "mother's
teaching," and the word translated *teaching* is *TORAH*,
which the KJV translates *law*. This law is not the recital of
commands given at Sinai, though it may be based on them.
It is simply teaching or instruction in godly behaviour.
TORAH is used in this sense several times in Proverbs,
usually where the *TORAH* is given by the parents. Whereas
the KJV translates this as *law*, the NIV uses the term *teaching*
in order to distinguish such parental instruction from the
Sinai code.

The corresponding Greek word **NOMOS** is also used in
different senses. It can simply mean the Old Testament, as in
Romans 3:19, 21; it can mean "the law of Moses," as in
Romans 5:13; or it can have the sense of "God's word," as in
1 Corinthians 15:56.

5. *The broadest use of the term* law *is the* **moral law.**

This is not identical with the Sinai code, although they often
coincide. For moral law was not invented at Sinai, nor even
first revealed then. There have always been moral absolutes,
certain standards of behaviour required by God. They come
from the holy and righteous nature of God himself and are
part of the divine image he stamped on man at creation.

> Adam had the spirit of the law impregnating his moral
> being; he had the mind of the Lawgiver himself given to bear
> rule within—hence not so properly a revelation of the law...as
> an inspiration from the Almighty, giving him understanding in

regard to what, as an intelligent and responsible being, it became him to purpose and do in life.[6]

These moral attributes therefore existed long before Sinai and the Ten Commandments. Man was always required to behave righteously and in this way to express his likeness to God. This comes out from time to time in Scripture, even in the books of the law themselves, for example, in Deuteronomy 10:12–13:

> And now, O Israel, what does the Lord your God ask of you but to fear the Lord your God, to walk in all his ways, to love him, to serve the Lord your God with all your heart and with all your soul, and to observe the Lord's commands and decrees, that I am giving you today for your own good?

The eternal, universal and general requirements of God are put before the specific duty of obeying the Law of Sinai. Micah 6:8 is similar:

> He has showed you, O man, what is good. And what does the Lord require of you? To do justly and to love mercy and to walk humbly with your God.

Even after the fall he retained a sense of right and wrong, and a conscience which convicted him when he went wrong and reminded him he was accountable to God for his behaviour.

The term is used in this sense in Romans 2:14–15 which speaks of

> ... Gentiles, who do not have the law [Sinai], do by nature the things required by the law, [who therefore] are a law for themselves even though they do not have the law, since they show the requirements of the law are written on their hearts.

Three of these uses of *law* refer to the Sinai code, but the expression "a law for themselves" clearly does not, since

---

[6] A.M. Fairbairn, *Revelation of the Law in Scripture* (Grand Rapids, Michigan: Zondervan, 1957) 48.

"the Gentiles do not have the law." It must therefore refer to something in their very nature: a sense of right and wrong, together with a sense of obligation to do right and avoid wrong. Notice it is not "the Law" but "the requirements of the law" that are "written on their hearts." All men do not know the Ten Commandments or other written laws, but they do know what is right or wrong, which corresponds to the written law. This concept is normally called "natural law" or "primary law" and has been taught by most theologians down the ages. This therefore is not the same as what Jeremiah predicted when he said that in the new covenant "I will put my law in their minds and write it on their hearts" (Jer. 31:33). This is not the innate sense of right and wrong but the revealed Word of God. Paul brings it in here

> to substantiate the charge that he brings against all mankind, both Jews and Gentiles, that by nature they are wholly in sin, and that God, being no respecter of persons, will judge one as well as the other. Lest any should think God's actions were unduly severe on the Gentiles, Paul establishes the truth that they too were not without some knowledge of his will.[7]

Natural law is original and universal, since it derives from man's creation in God's image. However, the fall of man altered this situation. Although he knows what is right and wrong he is always unable to perform the right and avoid the wrong, so that he does not universally and perfectly obey the natural law. However, this does not excuse him from the obligation or exempt him from judgment for failure. For one thing, his moral inability is his own fault, because it results from a free choice, as we see with Adam in Genesis 2:17. In secular life a man's inability

---

[7] Kevan, *The Moral Law*, 41.

to pay a debt does not excuse him from the obligation, since he himself freely chose to get into debt. For another thing the 'common grace' of God ensures that man continues to conform to it sufficiently to preserve a measure of orderliness in the world.

This innate moral sense of right and wrong still exists and has even survived post-modernism. A few years ago a survey was made of people's attitudes to the law of God under the title of "The Top Twenty Commandments." It is significant that the majority of the answers people came up with correspond either to the Decalogue or Christ's ethical teaching or the moral exhortations of the apostolic letters. The full list of the Top Twenty Commandments reads:

1. Treat others as you would like them to treat you.
2. Take responsibility for your actions.
3. Do not kill.
4. Be honest.
5. Protect and nurture children.
6. Do not steal.
7. Protect the environment.
8. Look after the vulnerable.
9. Never be violent.
10. Protect your family.
11. Respect your parents.
12. Appreciate what you have.
13. Enjoy life.
14. Be true to yourself.
15. Try your best.
16. Live within your means.
17. Look after your health.
18. Do not commit adultery.
19. Have no other gods but God.
20. Do nothing in excess.

Reason and conscience bear witness to this. Anyone who thinks rationally will agree that God's requirements are in accord with reason. The fact that a man may argue against them is due to the perversion of his mind through his fallen nature. Once his nature is enlightened and regenerated he will "approve what God wills—his good, pleasing and perfect will" (Rom. 12:2). To some extent conscience compensates for this and tells a man that, despite his reasoning, what God says is right. This will often result in a conflict between his mind and his will, as Paul describes in Romans 7.

This teaching is important in connection with the preaching of the gospel, which usually states that all who are not in Christ will perish. This raises the question as to whether it is just to condemn those who have never heard the gospel. The answer is that people are not condemned for not having heard the gospel, but for sinning against the light of nature, reason, and conscience. Although all have knowledge of right and wrong, none invariably practises right and rejects wrong. A fuller discussion of this can be found in *The Grace of Law* by E.F. Kevan.[8]

In addition to revealed Law (Sinai) there is also positive law. This is law which is not directed at a specific moral evil or virtue but is given purely as a test of obedience. The greatest example of this is the command God gave to Adam in Genesis 2:17 forbidding him to eat of "the tree of the knowledge of good and evil." There was nothing evil about the tree itself; the command was given to Adam to teach him to obey God implicitly and without question. It presupposed that evil already existed, and to avoid it Adam must affirm his unquestioning obedience to God. It was called "the tree

---

[8] E.F. Kevan, *The Grace of Law* (London: Carey Kingsgate Press, 1964) 52-62.

of the knowledge of good and evil" because if he obeyed good would result, but if he disobeyed he would experience evil and be constantly faced with a choice between good and evil, a condition which has devolved on us all. Positive law is thus closely connected with natural law. Man has a capacity to discern between good and evil and is faced with a choice between them. Even if he makes the right choice, his capacity to act on it is limited and he will be unable to obey it fully.[9]

The command of Genesis 2:17 is clearly of a different kind from that given to Adam and Eve at their creation:

> *Be fruitful and increase in number; fill the earth and subdue it. Rule over the fish of the sea and the birds of the air, and over every living creature that moves on the ground* (Gen. 1:28. See also Gen. 2:15).

These are not moral matters like the command not to eat of the tree of the knowledge of good and evil. This is not a test of obedience but rather an encouragement to explore and enjoy their creation and to employ their God-given powers. We shall find a similar difference between encouragements and commands in Chapter 10, "The Law and Holiness."

Along with all this goes the sense of *accountability* we feel for our behaviour, of which he speaks in Romans 1:32 and which Paul calls conscience in Romans 2:15. In 1 Corinthians 9:21 God's law is distinguished from the law (of Moses) and even from Christ's law. This can only mean God's eternal moral requirements. In Romans 6:15–18 we are told that, although we are not "under the law" we are obligated to a standard of righteousness which is equivalent to it—that is, God's eternal moral law.

William van Gemeren has written:

---

[9] Kevan, *op. cit.*, 69-77.

Philosophers and theologians have posited the existence of a moral order—or natural law—that reasonable human beings may discover. Some have explained this order as deriving from the will of God (e.g., Scotus and Ockham) and others as deriving from the essence of things (e.g., Aquinas).

John Calvin accepted the medieval concept of natural law:

The Westminster Divines agreed with Calvin that God had endowed Adam and Eve with the ability to develop a moral order and, thus, to live in harmony with God's will. This law was "a perfect rule of righteousness." If our first parents had obeyed it, they would have demonstrated a righteousness apart from the written law.[10]

So the *requirements of the law* are what I have termed the *moral absolutes*, that state of righteousness which the law of Moses was designed to promote in Israel. These are written, not on tablets of stone but on the heart, and therefore were there long before the Sinai code was written, both that which was written on the stone tablets (the Ten Commandments) and that which was subsequently written on whatever material was available. It is this aspect of the subject which will be taken up in the next chapter.

James 2:8 uses an interesting expression: "the royal law," which he defines as the law of love. This takes us right back to the original state of man after creation. His relationship with God was one of love (see Chapter 2), as was his relationship with Eve, his only 'neighbour.' Had the fall not occurred, this would have continued through the human race. When Christ came, he declared this as the whole purpose of the law—see Matthew 22:34–40. He who fulfilled the whole law in himself also fulfilled it in those he redeemed by restoring them to their original relationship of

[10] William A. van Gemeren, "The Law is the Perfection of Righteousness in Jesus Christ" in *Five Views on Law and Gospel* (Grand Rapids: Zondervan, 1999) 20-21.

love to God and man. The royal law is the law of the King restored in those who belong to his kingdom. This spirit of love is even more fundamental to the nature of man than the sense of right and wrong. James' words may therefore be taken as an example of this broad use of *law*.

So we must be careful to distinguish the moral law from the Sinai code. Some writers identify the Sinai law with the eternal moral law. "The law which is obligatory on the believer is the same in substance as the law of Moses."[11] This leaves open the question as to what particular laws were for Israel and what are for all people of all time. The Sinai law was for Israel during the theocracy, when the people of God were in their infancy (Gal. 4:3). In Christ, we have grown out of our infancy, and entered into "the full rights of sonship" (Gal. 4:4–5). This explains the elaborate system of punishments in the Sinai legislation. With young children punishments are more frequent than in older ones, for they are being trained in obedience.

---

[11] Kevan, *Grace of Law,* 158.

CHAPTER 2
LAW BEFORE THE LAW

"Before the law" is an expression Paul used in Romans 5:13, indicating how important it is in this matter to go back to the beginning. "Before the law was given sin was in the world." If this is so, sin must be more than breaking the law. This is what Paul goes on to say in Romans 5:13–14:

> But sin is not taken into account when there is no law. Nevertheless death reigned from the time of Adam to the time of Moses, even over those who did not sin by breaking a command, as did Adam.

The existence of death before the law shows there must have been sin, since death is "the wages of sin" (Rom. 6:23). This raises the question of what exactly comprised sin when there were no commands or laws to break.

Before the fall, man and God enjoyed a relationship of love and trust. God in his great **love** created man in his likeness and gave him the riches of his creation to enjoy (Gen. 1:28–30). Man was expected to feel and express his gratitude to God and to lead the other earthly creatures in rendering him praise, thus following the example of the heavenly creation, of whom we read

> the morning stars sang together and all the angels shouted for joy
> (Job 38:7)

Psalms such as Psalm 148 echo the anthem of that great choir which united earth and heaven, a unity broken by the fall, but which will be restored by Christ at the end of time (Eph. 1:10).

God also entrusted to man *the care of his creation* (Gen. 2:15). This included taking charge of the animals; the right to name them symbolised his authority over them (Gen. 2:19–20). Since one couple could only care for a limited area, they were told to *reproduce*, bear children and populate the earth (Gen. 1:28). The whole earth must be cultivated and cared for. These instructions are not commandments or laws, although they are grammatically in the imperative mood, but are more like encouragements to receive the gifts which God is offering them. They do not imply any disposition in man to disobey, or even the slightest reluctance to carry them out. They are more in the realm of teaching man what he is here for and encouraging him to fulfill his role, for in this he will find his greatest happiness. These entrustments showed him how special he was to God to be given favours such as even angels did not have. It was a truly beautiful relationship on both sides.

Then came the fall which resulted from Adam's disobedience to what God said in Genesis 2:17:

> *...you must not eat from the tree of the knowledge of good and evil, for when you eat of it you will surely die.*

This was the first sign of a dark cloud appearing in their relationship. But the sun still shines, for God reiterates his gift to man of everything the earth possessed (Gen. 2:16). However, a new situation has arisen which necessitates the warning God gives. Evil has appeared in the universe. Although not spelt out, it is clear that evil originated in the angelic creation. A glorious angel, perhaps the leading one, has aspired to the throne of God and thus become Satan, his *adversary*, as the name means. God foresaw that Satan would seek to recruit man on to his side, become his accuser (devil) and thus his destroyer (Apollyon).

God therefore warns Adam that he is in danger of being tempted to disobey him. The consequence of this will be death. Some think death was already happening in creation, since Adam does not ask for or receive any explanation of what to him was a novel condition. Be that as it may, death will mean far more for Adam than for any other creature. It will mean loss of his right to the tree of life. Man was not made to live on earth forever, but eventually to be elevated to the angelic sphere where he can behold the face of God, as the angels do. This was to happen without death, as it did for Enoch and Elijah. The way to avoid death was to continue in that attitude of loving, trusting obedience in which he had begun. The whole matter was encapsulated in a certain tree whose fruit was forbidden because it would open his eyes to "the knowledge of good and evil," which means, not a theoretical knowledge but the knowledge that comes from experience. He will be confronted by a choice between good and evil, between obeying and pleasing God or disobeying him and incurring his displeasure. The divided heart which will result is described by Paul in Romans 7.

This itself would be one form of death—the death of his loving and trusting relationship with God. This is demonstrated by what happens immediately on the act of disobedience, for Adam feels guilty and hides, and God comes to him not as a loving Father but an interrogator and judge. Adam's personality will experience division, and he will make wrong choices. This will damage the likeness to God in which he was first made. It will also affect his relationship with his fellow creatures. This appears immediately with Adam blaming Eve and implicitly God himself who had given him the woman. This conflict was perpetuated in their offspring, Cain and Abel, between whom a spirit of jealousy sprang up, leading to murder (Gen. 4:2–8). Furthermore, listening to Satan put him into the power of Satan, and he will have a constant battle between serving Satan and serving God.

These broken pieces in man's nature of being made in the image of God will not be put together again until Christ comes and restores love and trust on both sides. Meanwhile, the broken pieces must be clearly labelled to show man what he must and must not do if he is to continue to know anything of God's favour. Ultimately this will be done by the use of the words "You shall..." and "You shall not..." But this is still a long way off. Until it comes they must learn by bitter experience what to do and what to avoid. There is a sense in which Adam and Eve broke God's laws in the very act of disobedience which caused the fall. Their desire for equality with God was a kind of *idolatry*—of themselves! They committed *false testimony* when they twisted God's words about what he had forbidden. Certainly *covetousness* was present in Eve's desire for the fruit; and so we could go on through the Commandments.

Thus we find that all those actions specified as sinful at Sinai, especially the Ten Commandments, are committed between the fall and Sinai, usually with bitter consequences. This is in keeping with Paul's teaching in Romans 5:12–14. "Sin entered the world" through Adam and was transmitted to his descendants by imputation, as Paul puts it: "for all sinned," that is, sinned in Adam whose sin is imputed to all. But, says Paul, "sin is not taken into account where there is no law," for "sin is transgression of the law" or "lawlessness" (1 Jn. 3:4). Yet, Paul adds, "sin was in the world" before the law, not only in Adam but in his descendants. Moreover, "death reigned from Adam to Moses" because people were being punished for sin even though they had not broken a law or disobeyed a command, as Adam had. So there must have been some sort of law during the period from Adam to Moses or they would not have been convicted of sin and condemned to death as a punishment for sin. With this E.F. Kevan agrees:

It is a mistake to think of the moral law as something new, for it is as original as the natural law. The moral law existed long before the administration of it by Moses. Murder was a sin from the very beginning, as appears by God's words to Cain; indeed, so also was the very anger itself that precedes murder. Men, therefore, were never without the Law, nor ever shall be, and there is a sense in which it may truly be said that the Decalogue belongs to Adam, to Noah, to Abraham, to Christ, to the Apostles as well as to Moses.[12]

This *law* is that referred to in Chapter One, point five (*page 8*): "the law written in the heart," the sense of right and wrong and the conscience that creates guilt over wrong or approval over right. The narrative between the fall and the revelation of the law at Sinai demonstrates this. Every act condemned as sin at Sinai was committed by Adam and his descendants. However, the Westminster Confession [XIX.ii] goes straight from Eden to Sinai. It says that "This law (the so-called *covenant of works*) continued to be a perfect rule of righteousness," but fails to explain how it continued.

Paul Helm writes: "between Adam and Moses no explicit divine command was given."[13] But there were, he says,

...universally recognised divinely-endorsed norms in society which were written into the conscience.

These were about both what is good and what is evil. They were known from the earliest times, as God's words to Cain show:

...*if you do well, will you not be accepted? But if you do not do what is right, sin is crouching at the door.* (Gen. 4:6–7)

These norms were general—among Gentiles as well as the children of Abraham. They were not done out of explicit

---

[12] Kevan, *The Moral Law*, 62.

[13] Paul Helm, "The Use of the Mosaic Law in Society Today," an unpublished paper for the Affinity Conference in 2009.

obedience to God, but out of a sense of moral accountability. This is what is meant by "the fear of God," as used in Genesis 20:11. This is not obedience and love to God personally but awareness of a supernaturally imposed moral order, for the breach of which there is judgment. We can find examples of this in the Old Testament prior to Sinai.

Murder was committed by Cain and by Lamech (Gen. 4:23). The strong prohibition on it after the Flood, on pain of death, shows it was now endemic in the human race (Gen. 9:5–6). The **violence** that accompanies murder was particularly rife among the antediluvians (Gen. 6:11). **Tyranny** was also a mark of this period: Genesis 6:4. **Sexual sin** is exemplified by Lamech (Gen. 4:19) and by Lot's daughters (Gen. 19:30–38). Abraham was probably guilty of it too when he took Hagar (Gen. 16:1–4), even though it was at his wife's suggestion. There was a danger of its occurring when Pharaoh took Sarah (Gen. 12:10–20), also when Abimelech did a similar thing (Gen. 20:1–7). He clearly knew adultery was wrong (Gen. 20:6). Homosexuality was rife in Sodom and was the main cause of its judgment (Gen. 19:4–5). **Idolatry** was practised everywhere, and Abraham himself was a worshipper of other gods until God spoke to him (Josh. 24:2). In fact, in the world of his time there was scarcely any other form of worship.

There are also lesser sins: Abraham (Gen. 12:10–20), Isaac (Gen. 26:9–11) and Jacob and his mother (Gen. 27) were all guilty of **deceit,** as was Rachel (Gen. 31:34–35), who also **stole** from her father (Gen. 31:19). These acts can also be classed as **disrespect for parents**, later to be condemned in the fifth commandment. Ham, son of Noah, was also guilty of this sin (Gen. 9:22). None of these actions met with the approval of the writers and must have had consequences of varying seriousness.

On the positive side, there was some virtue and righteousness! Some of the ancients were commended by the writer of the letter to the Hebrews, especially Abel, Enoch and Noah (cf. Heb. 11:1–7).

> Before the law was given, the godly walked with the Lord, loved him and maintained order in the world. Enoch, Noah and Abraham are representatives of the heroes of faith who observed the moral law by practising a righteousness and blamelessness apart from the law.[14]

The records we have of them in Genesis bear this out. Also, since it was the later patriarchs who declined into wickedness we must assume that the earlier ones who are recorded in Genesis 5 lived righteously and were rewarded with long lives; Job was said to be "blameless and upright" (Job 1:1) and his righteous manner of life is described in Job 29, even though it comes from his own mouth. His friends' attempts to convict him of sin carry no weight; he was as good as they, and they were certainly upholders of morality. Abraham is also said to have "kept laws" (Gen. 26:5). van Gemeren writes:

> Abraham obeyed [*šm'*] me and kept [*šmr*] my requirements [*mišmeret*], my commands [*miswâ*], my decrees [*huqqâ*] and my laws [*tôrâ*] (26:5). The choice of nouns (*miswâ, huqqâ, tôrâ*) and verbs (*šm', šmr*) is significant in that they anticipate the revelation at Mount Sinai.[15]

Prior to Sinai God was worshipped by sacrifice, though there is no record of his actually prescribing it. Exodus 3:18, 4:23, 5:1, 3 are instances of this, in addition to which he was worshipped by words and music: Exodus 15:1–18. As we draw nearer to Sinai we find God beginning to prepare the way for a new stage. It is he who orders the keeping of the Passover (Ex. 12–13) which is therefore called a *law* in

---

[14] van Gemeren, *Five Views on Gospel and Law*, 19.

[15] Ibid, 20.

Exodus 13:9. Then, as they approach the mountain, we find the closest anticipation of all—the honouring of the seventh day as a holy Sabbath, which made it necessary for them to gather twice as much manna on the day before: Exodus 16:22–25. When they attempted to collect manna on the Sabbath, they found none (Ex. 16:27). God was starting to discipline them "with commands and instructions" (Ex. 16:28). That this is centred on the law of the Sabbath is significant, for it will be the Sabbath that will form an important sign of the covenant relationship between God and Israel: See Exodus 31:16 and Ezekiel 20:12–20.

Sinai was thus the re-establishing of a relationship of love and trust, as far as it could go before Christ. The law was a holding operation, or, as Paul said, it acted as a pedagogue, a male servant who had the task of keeping the children of the family under control until they were mature enough to enjoy the freedom of sons: Galatians 4:1–3. The people of the old covenant were in the infancy of the church and needed rules to keep them in order until the Holy Spirit took over this role. But it was only temporary, since it did not restore the relationship between God and man to the pre-fall standard, and in any case only applied to one tiny nation.

It was to be the coming of Christ which would restore this relationship. He brought the love of God down to man and re-awoke the spirit of trust and love in his heart. In this way he restored that higher morality which existed before the fall and had not required laws. So Christ summarised the whole law as *love* (cf. Matt. 22:34–40), as did his apostles, for example, Paul in Romans 13:10, Galatians 5:14, Galatians 6:2, and James 2:8. His perfect law is seen in Matthew 5 (the Sermon on the Mount) which gets to the heart of each matter and ends with the call to love as the way to "be perfect" (Matthew 5:43–48). To say that "love is the fulfilment of the law" (Rom. 13:10) does not mean that love replaces law but that it gives us a heart to do willingly and gladly what law requires.

The highest expression of all is in Christ himself—his character and his relationship with God. Lest this should sound as though God has become a less awesome and exalted being than hitherto, we also find the idea of the fear of God in the sense of awe and reverence just as prominent in the New as in the Old Testament. See, for example, Romans 3:8, 2 Corinthians 7:1 and 1 Peter 1:7. All this proves the truth of Paul's words in Romans 5:13 that, "before the law sin was in the world."

Thus the individual commandments (apart from the fourth) were all in operation from the beginning, but were not made into a written covenant document until Moses. This is why the phrase *the Law* (in the singular) is not used before Sinai. It is to this we now turn.

CHAPTER 3
THE LAW OF MOSES

In the time of Moses those moral absolutes described in the last chapter came to be codified and written down at Mount Sinai, along with many other lesser rules. From that time on, the word 'law' in the Bible usually refers to those laws given to Moses on Mount Sinai. This chapter is therefore about the third of the five senses in which the term is used in the Bible and occurs most frequently.

Where found

This law is to be found in Exodus 20–40, parts of Leviticus and Numbers, and most of Deuteronomy. It would appear that after the basic regulations were given at Sinai, further rules were given by God from time to time during the journey of Israel to the Promised Land. It appears in its final form in Deuteronomy.

The Question of Three Categories

The particular laws themselves vary considerably. Some concern the Israelites' relationship with God, some their treatment of each other and some go into vast detail about forms of worship, along with the buildings to be used and those officiating at the services. Along with the laws appropriate punishments for breaking them were specified.

Yet, although so vast and varied, they form one body called *the Law*. It is true the term is sometimes used in the plural, but the number of occasions in which it is spoken of simply as **the** *Law* indicates that it was thought of as one whole. Every part, every particular law, carried the same authority. However, since at least the time of Thomas Aquinas (13th century) it has been customary to divide the

Law into three categories: moral, civil (or judiciary) and ceremonial. Aquinas saw scriptural justification for the distinction in Deuteronomy 6:1, where three different terms are used: *commands, decrees* and *laws,* referring to moral, ceremonial and judicial laws. However, it is difficult to give them an equivalent significance in other places where these terms occur.

Calvin is usually regarded as the source of the view that the laws of Moses fall into three categories. However, this is not discussed until the final chapter of Book IV of *The Institutes*[16] in connection with Civil Government (ch.xx.15) and there are only three brief paragraphs in which he distinguishes the moral, ceremonial and judicial laws. By the moral laws he appears to mean the Ten Commandments, for although he does not use that phrase he states that it has "two heads, one of which commands us to worship God…, the other to embrace men with sincere affection." This sounds like what are usually called "the two tables of the law." This is "the eternal rule of righteousness, prescribed for all nations and times."

"The ceremonial law was the tutelage of the Jews with which it seemed good to the Lord to train his people, as it were in their childhood, until the fullness of the time should come." It appears that the judicial law was also confined to the Jews, for he says "it was given to them for civil government." This means the two latter categories are now obsolete, but the former, the Ten Commandments, are still in operation. However, there is no discussion of the rest of the Mosaic law outside the Commandments. Yet this is the agreed view of Puritan theologians and many Reformed

---

[16] John Calvin, *Institutes of the Christian Religion,* ed., John T. McNeill, (Philadelphia, The Westminster Press, 1960).

teachers since then. However, more recent Reformed theologians have come up with alternatives.

Obviously there are laws that are moral in the sense of defining right and wrong behaviour applying to all people for all time, and for which they are accountable to God. But taking a section of the law of Moses (the Ten Commandments) and calling it "the Moral Law" is not done in Scripture. This is a theological rather than a biblical term used in doctrinal statements such as the Westminster Confession of Faith (XIX.iii, v). Also the word *moral* is normally used in contrast to *immoral*. However, in this context it is used in contrast to *ceremonial*, which is misleading. Similarly, there are laws which apply to community living for Israel in the Promised Land, for which the people were accountable to the judicial authorities. In the same way there are detailed and elaborate rules about the conduct of the ceremonies prescribed by God. In these senses there are indeed moral, judicial and ceremonial laws.

However, nowhere in Scripture is this three-fold division mentioned.

> … it is not self-evident that either OT or NT writers neatly classify OT laws in those categories in such a way as to establish continuity and discontinuity on the basis of such distinctions.[17]

Everywhere, in the books of Moses and the prophets, the histories and the writings, the Old Testament and the New, all are lumped together as *the Law*. Dr Kevan, although he accepted the threefold distinction, did so only cautiously:

> The history of the Old Testament reveals that *torah* had a threefold character: it was moral, ceremonial and judicial. It would not be correct to separate the Law into three divisions—

---

[17] D.A. Carson, *From Sabbath to Lord's Day*, 68.

for the Mosaic Law is one inseparable whole—but there are certainly some differences of character to be seen.[18]

All three types are present in the Sinai code but nowhere distinguished by these names. "The Book of the Law" (probably Exodus 20:22–23:19) contains them all, as does Leviticus 19. In Leviticus 19:5 a ceremonial commandment concerning a fellowship offering is juxtaposed with more moral laws. The Sabbath is placed among the moral laws in the Decalogue, whereas in Leviticus 23 and Numbers 28 it is placed with other ceremonies.

It seems, therefore, that the detailed laws following the Decalogue from Exodus 20:22 are the application of the Ten Commandments. This means that laws about worship—the ceremonial law—for example, in Exodus 20:22–26, 23:14–19 and Exodus 25–31—are the application of the second commandment for the people of Israel. This makes the second commandment ceremonial as well as moral. Likewise the detailed laws about the Sabbath, regarded as the ceremonial law, are the application of the fourth commandment, which is also, therefore, not only moral but ceremonial.

Similarly, the laws in Exodus 21–22 concerning the treatment of slaves, murder and manslaughter, and the restitution of property, which are regarded by advocates of the threefold distinction as the 'civil code' or 'judicial law' have a strong flavour of morality. How then can we make these rigid distinctions?

Concerning the judicial law the Westminster Confession uses the phrase *general equity*:

> To them (the people of Israel) also, as a body politick, he gave sundry judicial laws, which expired together with the

---

[18] E.F. Kevan, *Keep the Commandments* (London: Tyndale, 1964) 14.

state of that people, not obliging any other now, further than the general equity thereof may require (XIX.iv).

This seems to mean 'natural justice' or 'that which is fair.' In legal matters it would be impossible to legislate for every eventuality, so that many things have to be left to reason and conscience. Used in this sense the principle seems to go back to Aristotle and can be found in his book on ethics.

In theological matters the use is similar. It is a principle to be applied to situations which cannot be covered by specific laws without producing a book of vast size. The Jews seem to have attempted this with their Mishnah, which had to be complemented with the Talmud. In any case, as David Dickson pointed out, Christians are told to keep the laws of their own country, which, unlike Israel, is not a theocracy. Christ seems to have done this when he framed the Golden Rule (Luke 6:31): individual conscience will decide how to apply this. It is also similar to Paul's distinction between the letter and the spirit of the law in 2 Corinthians 3:6.

However, the judicial laws of the Sinai code are still useful to us, provided we observe the intention behind them. The famous parapet law of Deuteronomy 22:8 is intended to lay the responsibility for the safety of others on the individual. It would be good if our Health and Safety legislators bore this in mind!

The three categories are never mentioned by Jesus and the apostles, who only ever talk of "the law." Jesus quoted from the so-called civil law and applied it to his description of the church in Matthew 18:16. In Galatians 5:3 Paul says that to be circumcised puts someone under an obligation to "the whole law," which must include the moral as well as the ceremonial regulations. James also uses the expression "the whole law" in James 2:10. His dire warning that "whoever … stumbles at one point is guilty of breaking all of it" strongly confirms the unity of the Law. Making the threefold distinction enabled the Puritans to speak of "universal law" or "entire obedience to all parts of the law without exception."[19] Yet even they would want to excuse us from such laws as the food laws, which they did by relegating them to the ceremonial law and which they claimed is now abolished. This means their idea of 'entire obedience' has to be severely qualified. Nowhere is there any authority for saying some were national and some universal, some temporary and some eternal. People are either under the law or not under the law. They were not under some parts of the law, such as the moral and not under others, such as the judicial or ceremonial. If a time came when they ceased to be under the law, then they ceased to be under it all, not just parts of it. In any case, since all laws come from a holy and righteous God, all must be moral in the sense that to disobey any command of God is immoral. D.A. Carson has well said:

> I would want to argue that what God approves is fundamentally right and what he forbids is fundamentally wrong, and in that case, when God approved certain ceremonial sacrifices in the Old Testament, people were *morally* bound to practise them. Again, if God forbade certain *civil* practices in the Old Testament, it would have been *immoral* to proceed with them, just because it was God who prohibited them.[20]

Why was the Law given?

The big question is not how do we divide up the Law but **to whom does it apply?** Does it apply to everyone or only to Israel? Does it apply to the Christian, and does the fact of whether he was a Jew or Gentile before becoming a

[19] Kevan, *Grace of Law*, 179.

[20] D.A. Carson, *Sermon on the Mount* (Carlisle, UK: Paternoster, 1978) 39-40.

Christian affect the matter? The best way to approach this aspect of the matter is to address the question **why was the Law given?** Clearly it was not to show what is right or wrong, since this was already known (see Chapter 2). The Law did not invent morality. What then did it do?

Covenant

The reason God gave the Law is very clearly stated: it formed the terms and conditions of **the covenant** God made with Israel. "A covenant in Scripture is a relationship based on a promise with obligations and signs."[21] The Sinai covenant did not replace the promise to Abraham of the gift of righteousness by faith (which is for all who in any age believe the gospel: Gen. 15:6, Rom. 4:4–24, Gal. 3:10–19). Nor did it replace the covenant between God and Abraham to make a special nation belonging to God from his offspring (Gen. 17:1–8). It was a covenant made with those who were officially adopted as his people as "a kingdom of priests and a holy nation" at Sinai (Ex. 19:5–6). It was a legal covenant made exclusively with Israel:

> The Mosaic covenant *as a covenant* is exclusive to the Jews.[22]

This was to remain in force until the new covenant was made in Christ, "the messenger of the covenant" (Mal. 3:1), that is, the new covenant. The prophets reveal how Israel broke the conditions of the Sinai covenant and thus forfeited its blessings.

They also spoke of a new covenant, a covenant of promise. This will go beyond the covenant with Abraham, for instead of the sign of circumcision in the flesh (or even in

---

[21] Christopher Bennett, "The Use of the Mosaic Law in the New Testament Church", in *The End of the Law,* Affinity Conference Paper, Bridgend, Affinity, 2009.

[22] D.R. de Lacey, *From Sabbath to Lord's Day,* 163.

the heart) it promises a new heart. When this occurs, the covenant of the law will have been fulfilled.

The covenant of Sinai is important as a holding operation because it proclaims:

- God's holiness.

- His people's commitment to obedience.

- A way to cover their failures until the Saviour comes.

This latter aspect is not absent from Sinai, as is seen in the way the Decalogue begins: "I am the Lord **your** God" — he is **their** God, bound to them by covenant (as the ceremony at Sinai shows). This is why mention is made in the first commandment of his redemption of the people from Egypt which made them his people. The tablets were housed in the ark under the mercy seat to pledge the continuance of his love until the fulfilment in the new covenant in Christ.

Law in Scripture is anything that requires obedience from God's people, which includes the threat of punishment for disobedience. The promise, on the other hand, calls for faith. Both of these run through Old and New Testaments alike. The Decalogue is a covenant of law, and the covenant with Abraham is a covenant of promise. The requirement of circumcision was not a condition, which would make it a law covenant, but a sign of the promise. This is what Paul meant when he used the expression "until Christ" (Gal. 3:24 NIV mg). The promise is of the coming of the Messiah to bring in his kingdom for which the Old Testament prepares, and the fulfilment is in his actual arrival to establish his kingdom. This means that the Old Testament must be understood via the New Testament and not vice versa, as Ephesians 3:4–5 says:

> ...*the mystery of Christ, which was not made known to men in other generations as it has now been revealed by the Spirit in God's holy apostles and prophets.*

The law has no place in making sons of Abraham because the Abraham covenant is of faith and precedes the law. Its fulfilment is in Christ, which means that those who are one with Christ are sons of Abraham and not under the law. It is significant that in condemning incest in 1 Corinthians 5 and sexual misconduct generally in 1 Corinthians 6, Paul does not appeal to the law but to the believer's union with Christ: 1 Corinthians 6:15–20. Paul, in Galatians 4, illustrated the difference between the covenants by comparing Hagar and Sarah. Hagar was the servant or slave, not the wife. Therefore her children were also slaves (Gal. 4:24). They represent Israel under the law (Gal. 4:21). Believers under the new covenant are free.

It was at Sinai that he first declared Israel to be his special chosen people:

> *Although all the earth is mine, you will be for me a kingdom of priests and a holy nation* (Ex. 19:5–6).

It was at Sinai that he first put this relationship into the form of a covenant:

> *Now if you obey me fully and keep my covenant, then out of all nations you will be my treasured possession* (Ex. 19:5).

> *The Lord our God made a covenant with us in Horeb. It was not with our fathers that the Lord made this covenant, but with us* (Deut. 5:2–3).

The Ten Commandments are at the heart of the covenant:

> *He declared to you his covenant, the Ten Commandments, which he commanded you to follow, and then wrote them on two stone tablets* (Deut. 4:13).

> *And he wrote on the tablets the words of the covenant–the Ten Commandments* (Ex. 34:28).

They are therefore particularly strong in covenant language. The preface (Ex. 20:1) calls him "the Lord **your** God," theirs by covenant, for he brought them out of Egypt to be his own. The Sinai covenant is therefore addressed to the redeemed. The second commandment uses the same phrase and stresses the exclusivity of this relationship. The third, fourth and fifth commandments likewise call him "**your** God." The fifth also alludes to the covenant promise to give them the land, for which he took them out of Egypt.

> *That you may live long in the land the Lord your God is giving you* (Ex. 20:12).

When it was written down it was called "the Book of the Covenant" (Ex. 24:3–8). It was sealed, authenticated, and brought into operation by having blood sprinkled on it and placing it side by side with the ark of the covenant (Deut. 31:24–26). The ark of the covenant was so called because it housed the covenant document, the Ten Commandments. This was a *testimony* (as the document is sometimes called) to the fact that Israel remained God's chosen people as long as they obeyed his commandments. Jesus was born under this covenant (Gal. 4:4), as proved by his eighth day circumcision. He remained under it during his earthly life and died under its curse (Gal. 3:13), proving that he took on both the law's demands and its punishments. The blood he shed ended the old covenant and inaugurated the new covenant for believers.

Placing the covenant document in the ark signified on the one hand the pledge of God to honour it, and on the other the obligation of the people to keep it on pain of death. To break a law was to break the covenant (Lev. 26:15). This applied especially to certain laws: circumcision (Gen. 17:14), as Moses found to his cost when God threatened to kill him for failing to circumcise his son (Ex. 4:24–26), idolatry (Deut. 31:16, 20), false worship (Ezek. 44:7), marriage (Mal. 2:10) and particularly the Sabbath (Ex. 31:13–17, Ezek. 20:12–20). When the covenant was renewed at the dedication of the rebuilt walls of Jerusalem after the return from Babylon, particular stress was laid on the Sabbath (see Neh. 10:31).

So, at the end of their journey and at the end of his life, Moses summarized both the blessings of obedience (God's promises) and the curses of disobedience (his punishments). These were to be recited at a gathering of the tribes as soon as they had entered the Promised Land (see Deut. 27–28).

Uniqueness and Perfection

The law given to Moses on Sinai is **unique** in human history. This was what Moses tried to impress on the people shortly before he left them to make the final stage of their journey (Deuteronomy 4:5–8).

Other nations struggle to draw up a code of laws that will be effective in maintaining order and controlling crime without being overbearing or unjust. Some are so concerned about human rights that they leave little room for just punishments to be inflicted on the criminal. Others are so set on keeping the lid on disorderly behaviour that they deprive their citizens of their freedoms. Such was the famous Draco[23] of ancient date. Those who seek to strike a balance between these two principles, as our own society does, never attain to the final form of law, but are constantly repealing old legislation or framing new laws. If we ever arrive at a perfect code there will be hardly anything for Parliament to do!

But the code God gave Moses on Sinai was never added to or taken from. Indeed, this was absolutely forbidden: Deuteronomy 4:2. The law not to change the Law, we might say, put the finishing touch on the code. So we never read of the authorities in Israel ever making changes to what was revealed at Sinai. They never arrive at a situation in which

---

[23] A seventh century B.C. Athenian lawyer who revised the laws of Athens with such severity that death was the penalty for almost every crime. It is from his name we get the phrase, "Draconian laws."

they feel they can dispense with a particular law, nor did circumstances ever arise which required the framing of a new law. In fact each king, when he came to the throne, was required to make his own personal copy of the law as it stood: Deuteronomy 17:18–20. This continued right through the old covenant period.

This is clear testimony to its perfection. Paul acknowledged this in Romans 7:12. This is why he says his "inner being delighted in it" (Rom. 7:22). But this may imply that outwardly "in his flesh" he found it difficult to observe perfectly. To keep a perfect law perfectly requires a theocracy. Israel had it, we do not. This is why the law of Moses cannot be imposed on all indiscriminately and written into the constitution of a nation. Only theocracies like Iran and Saudi Arabia can do this. It also explains the thrust of the ministry of priests, Levites and prophets. The Levites were to go among the people teaching the Law; the prophets were to denounce their failure to keep it and threaten dire punishments from God if this continued, and the priests' ministry was to provide forgiveness for those who confessed their failure and sought pardon. But never is there any criticism of the Law itself. It is in these ways we see the uniqueness of this Law: it came in the form of a covenant, given by God directly—something unknown in the world before or since. The nearest to it in the ancient world is the famous *Code of Hammurabi*, which predates Sinai by two or three centuries.

The manner in which the Law was revealed

But there are other ways in which we see the uniqueness of the Law, and that is in the manner in which it was revealed.

Firstly, the Lord secured from the people in advance a promise that they will obey it in its entirety:

The people all responded together, "We will do everything the Lord has said" (Ex. 19:8).

This is hardly normal! A government will usually put its constitution either to the vote of the people directly in a referendum, or to their representatives in Parliament. Tyrannical governments who short circuit the process and just impose their laws do not bother to get a promise of obedience out of the people, but simply threaten them with dire punishments if they fail to comply.

Secondly, God sealed off the mountain on which he was to appear when he revealed his Law: Exodus 19:12–13. The Law-giver was not merely one with authority and power, but a God of holiness whom sinners were not fit to approach. About this they must be very clear. As sinners they were not qualified to frame laws or assess them. Indeed it was because they were sinners that God was giving them laws at all. The Law *defines* what is sinful (cf. 1 Jn. 3:4), and so acquaints us with our state before God: "by the Law is the knowledge of sin." At the same time the Law *restrains* sin; it kept the Israelites from breaking out into the vile behaviour of the Gentiles during the period before Christ (Gal. 3:23–24). Above all, it shows the radical difference between man and God. Man cannot even occupy the same ground as God when he comes.

Thirdly, the people had to undergo a ritual cleansing (Ex. 19:14). It was not enough for them to distance themselves from the place where God was to appear. They will still be near enough to experience the phenomena that accompanied his appearance and even to hear the sound of his voice, although they may not have been able to discern what he was saying. Nor was their cleansing and consecration merely a ritual—their behaviour had to correspond to it, so they were to "abstain from sexual relations" (Ex. 19:15).

Fourthly, and most powerfully, were the supernatural phenomena that preceded God's giving of the Law: Exodus 19:16. As if this were not terrifying enough when they heard it from the tents, Moses led them out of the camp to the foot of the mountain to experience the phenomena as closely as possible. When they reached the foot of the mountain, it became even more terrifying, see Exodus 19:17–19.

At this point the Lord descended to the top of Sinai and Moses went up to him (Ex. 19:20).

But he was still not ready to declare his law! Moses must first warn the people not to approach any nearer. For the vast majority this was the last thing they wanted to do! However, knowing that human curiosity knows no bounds, this final warning had to be given. If they disregarded it, he twice says "the Lord will break out against them" (Ex. 19:22, 24).

This typifies the whole ethos of the Law. It proclaims the holiness of God and the sinfulness of man, and thus the separation of God from man. Israel was specially favoured above all peoples, but they were still tainted with the sin that infects the whole of humanity, so that it can in no way come near to God. This is probably the chief thing the Law has to say to us, as Joshua said later in Joshua 24:19–20.

Abiding Value

Yet it is not **all** that can be said. While it was all very terrifying, yet even that was a privilege afforded to no other nation. The gods of the other nations were dumb idols and could speak neither words of terror or comfort. But the God who entered into covenant relationship with Israel at Sinai was altogether other, as Moses sought to impress on the people when he spoke to them for the last time from the plains of Moab: Deuteronomy 4:32–40.

So the Law was given "that it may go well with you." It may have been **revealed** in a terrifying way, but down the years it could be a great blessing. It was to govern them in their life in the Promised Land for generations to come. It was perfect, requiring no addition or alteration. So it must have abiding value. Though, as we shall see, we Christians are no longer in the covenant of Sinai and therefore not "under the law," it still has a value for us and for everyone; there is even glory in it.

First and foremost, the Law reveals much about **the character of God.**

His Sovereignty. God's sovereignty means his right as Creator of all things to order and dispose of them according to his own pleasure. This attribute is basic to his law since it is this that gives him the right to command and to require obedience.

> God has the right to command because he is the source and end of all things. His sovereignty derives from the Creator-creature relationship and, since man was made in the moral image of God, moral obedience immediately becomes due from such a creature to his maker.[24]

His Justice. Whatever may be said against the Law, it cannot be accused of injustice. Its punishments are often considered harsh, for example, the *lex talionis* (eye for eye, tooth for tooth) but they are perfectly just. The Law, therefore, could not save sinners, which was the mistake made by Israel, as the New Testament makes clear when it teaches mercy and salvation through Christ in the new covenant, the gospel. Gouging out the eye of someone who has done that to someone else may be thought of as cruel, even barbaric, but it is just. The more positive requirements of the Law may appear unnecessarily rigorous, for example,

---

[24] Kevan, *The Grace of Law*, 48.

the laws against mixtures: seeds, textiles, etc., but they cannot be called unjust. Why is it we find it so difficult to get our sentencing right, with the result that a murderer may get away with a shorter sentence than one guilty of a lesser crime? Is it not because we are unrighteous people, we are biased and prejudiced, we have other things beside justice on our agenda, which make us think more about the person than his crime? We also over-react when a certain crime is in danger of reaching epidemic proportions. Harsh punishments are brought in to stamp it out, yet more serious crimes, because they are not so rampant, are treated with less severity. The Law's system of punishments was based fairly and squarely on the principle of retribution, and it clearly worked well, for they had no need of prisons!

His Holiness. The laws relating to clean and unclean food seem incomprehensible to us, but their purpose is clearly stated in Leviticus 11:44–45:

> *I am the Lord your God; consecrate yourselves and be holy, because I am holy. Do not make yourselves unclean by any creature that moves about on the ground. I am the Lord who brought you out of Egypt to be your God; therefore be holy because I am holy.*

These dietary laws are to show his people that the God who has chosen them is a God who is holy—*wholly other* than his creatures, and makes distinctions between what is acceptable to him and what is unacceptable. Those who are his must be like him—holy—and therefore make the same distinctions. The same attribute lies behind the laws relating to diseases in Leviticus 12–15.

His Compassion. Although much of the law seems stringent, there is compassion in it. Numbers 9:1–14 suggests that two Passovers were held in two months because some missed the first one through ceremonial uncleanness. This shows God as a God who is more interested in people than rules. The poor are to be given special consideration:

When you reap the harvest of your land, do not reap to the very edges of the field or gather the gleanings of your harvest. Do not go over your vineyard a second time or pick up the grapes that have fallen. Leave them for the poor and the alien. I am the Lord your God (Lev. 19:9–10).

Nor is advantage to be taken of the deaf and blind:

Do not curse the deaf or put a stumbling-block in front of the blind, but fear your God. I am the Lord (Lev. 19:14).

The aged are to be respected:

Rise in the presence of the aged, show respect for the elderly, and revere your God. I am the Lord (Lev. 19:32).

Foreigners living among them must be treated well:

When an alien lives with you in your land, you must treat him as one of your native-born. Love him as yourself, for you were aliens in Egypt. I am the Lord your God (Lev. 19:33).

His Mercy. Much of the law concerns sin. While it defines and condemns sin it also makes provision for its pardon. The whole sacrificial system, which forms a large part of Leviticus, is with a view to obtaining forgiveness and remission of God's punishment.

Here is a principle we can follow in the present day: to apply the character of God (about which we under the new covenant know more than those under the old covenant) to our lives and situations. For we, Christians, are also called to be holy:

But just as he who called you is holy, so be holy in all you do; for it is written: "Be holy, because I am holy" (1 Pet. 1:15–16).

How do we do this? In the same way: apply the attributes of God to our lives and behaviour.

Secondly, the Law exalts the whole idea of **order in society**. Because by nature we are each in a disordered state (James 4:1), disorder tends to mark our conduct in general and our treatment of each other in particular. The Law was designed to obviate this. It anticipated the ways in which human beings aggravate each other and forbade them, on pain of an appropriate punishment. If only the people had valued their Law more, been better acquainted with it and observed it, there would have been no brutality, theft or ill-treatment of any kind among them, and they would have been a shining light to the nations around them. Paul seems to be referring to this aspect in 1 Timothy 1:9–10.

It is considerations like this that explain that great eulogy on the law which is the subject of Psalm 119. The psalmist goes into raptures over it with expressions like "O how I love your law; I meditate on it all day long!" (Ps. 119:97). When **we** read such words we tend to substitute *Bible* for *law* and exult in the blessing we derive from the Word of God. However, the psalmist did not have the Bible we have. At best he had the Pentateuch, some of the early histories and possibly Job. In any case, when he said "Law" he meant what we have been considering in this section, for his synonyms for it are terms like *precepts, statutes* and *commandments.* None of these remotely describes the narrative or poetic books. When **we** read the law sections we tend not to be moved to rejoicing. Evidently he saw something more in them than we do—probably the gloriously just, holy, compassionate and merciful God who gave it to them. They had something other nations lacked and therefore strove for, but never arrived at: a perfectly just legal system. They had something unique, and it signified a unique relationship with the one true God; they were actually in covenant with him—he gave them promises and was faithful to them! We could, however, say there is something in our new covenant gospel which corresponds to the old covenant law—the will of God. The Law was the expression of God's will for his people in those days. But to us God has revealed more of his will in his gospel. So Paul, after he had outlined the gospel in Romans 1–11, says Romans 12:2:

> ...*be transformed by the renewing of your mind. Then you will be able to test and approve what God's will is—his good, pleasing and perfect will.*

"The will of God" covers both law and gospel and wins our total approval. However, there is something else, of which they would have only been vaguely aware, but which is far clearer to us.

Thirdly, it **points to Christ.** No one in Israel managed to conform to the Law in its entirety; even the greatest among them were flawed. This is what David complained of in his Psalm 14:2–3. But it applied equally to him, for he broke the 6th, 7th and 10th commandments in just one episode—the matter of Bathsheba. The OT raises the question: will anyone ever come along who will be perfectly law-abiding? Yes, Jesus of Nazareth, who was not only "born under the law," but kept all its tenets (Matt. 5:17–18). When his trial was held, no one came up with any evidence that he had broken a single law of God or man. Charges had to be trumped up and false witnesses bribed.

But the most amazing thing of all was that he obeyed the law perfectly **in order to set us free from its demands**. The Law was only "until Christ" (Gal. 3:24). The words "to lead us to" are not in the Greek, and *to* should be translated *until*. "Christ is the end of the Law" (Rom. 10:4), its regime ends with him, as he himself claimed: it "will not pass away until all is accomplished" (Mat. 5:18)—and it was!—by him!

More to follow on this! Chapter 5 will be given to the subject of "The Law's Purpose."

CHAPTER 4
THE TEN COMMANDMENTS

It was stated in Chapter 1 that, before any law or laws came to be written on stone or any other materials, "the requirements of the law" were "written on the heart" (Rom. 2:15). Man had a moral nature derived from his creation in the image of a moral God. This led on to the examples in Chapter 2 of how this nature revealed itself. Through disobedience to God man became a fallen creature and did many things of which God disapproved and which revealed how sin had become endemic in his nature. There are many instances of this in the Bible between the fall and Sinai. Although no specific laws against these practices had been revealed at the time, they were still sins, as Paul teaches in Romans 5:13–14: "before the law sin was in the world." The proof of this was death which "reigned from Adam to Moses, even over those who did not sin by breaking a command, as Adam did." This did not mean that man became absolutely evil; in fact we find examples of righteous behaviour in the period before Sinai. Chapter 3 took us to the time when God spoke and revealed his will for human behaviour in the law he issued on Mount Sinai.

At the heart of this law lie the Ten Words or Commandments. Indeed it is with these that the Law of Moses begins. It is time, then, to look at the place of the Ten Commandments in God's revelation of law.

The Codification of Sins

The Ten Commandments did not invent morality. The phrase *Ten Commandments* is used only three times in the Old Testament: in Exodus 34:28, Deuteronomy 4:13, and

Deuteronomy 10:4, and not at all in the New Testament. But
they did clarify and summarise the behaviour God expects
of man. All of these except the fifth and part of the fourth are
couched in negative terms. If there are corresponding
virtues, they are implied rather than stated. The
Westminster Larger Catechism spells these sins and duties
out at great length, which is good, although it is not the way
they were originally given. Basically, what they did and still
do is to set forth clearly in short simple language what
constituted sin in human beings. So we are not surprised to
find that what they prohibit are actions of which humans
were guilty before God spoke at Sinai.

The first commandment (Ex. 20:3) forbids idolatry:
having "other gods before (or besides) me." To acknowledge
other gods along with God is just as sinful as to have other
gods exclusively. Between Babel and the call of Abraham
idolatry was almost universal. The only exceptions we know
are Melchizedek, king of Salem, who was "priest of God
Most High" (*El Elyon*, Gen. 14:18–20), and possibly Job who
may have lived at this time, though the date cannot be
established. Abraham lived during the Sumerian civilisation
which, according to the archaeologists, worshipped sun,
moon and stars. This is probably what Joshua referred to
when he said that "Terah, father of Abraham and Nahor,
worshipped other gods" (Josh. 24:2). Abraham, whom God
"blessed" (Gen. 12:1–3) therefore lived the first half of his life
under God's curse. Along with the worship of the heavenly
bodies went the worship of living creatures (Rom. 1:22, 25).
The people of Israel also worshipped other gods during their
time in Egypt (Ezek. 20:7–8).

The second commandment (Ex. 20:4–6) forbids image-
worship. The ancients not only worshipped the heavenly
bodies and living creatures but made images of them (idols)
to bring them near and offer sacrifices to them. Laban, father

of Rachel and Leah, had "household gods" (Gen. 31:9) which Rachel stole when she left home with Jacob, and which Laban demanded back. In Egypt, where Jacob and his family came to live and which became home to their descendants for 400 or so years, idolatry and image-worship were rife. The host of heaven and many living creatures were sacred to the Egyptians. How far the Israelites became involved in this we are not told, but no doubt this is where they learned how to make the golden calf which became such a curse to them during the revelation of the law at Sinai (Ex. 32).

The third commandment (Ex. 20:7) forbids the misuse of God's name. Since for a long period of time the Lord's name was unknown to the vast majority of people, we can hardly expect examples of its misuse to be numerous. This applies particularly to what we today call blasphemy: using God's name as a curse or expletive. This may have occurred but, since Scripture does not on the whole record casual conversation in which most of what we call swearing or blasphemy is uttered, we can hardly expect to find occurrences of it there. The Scripture only sets down remarks that are significant and important. It will be among his own people who know his name that these are to be found, and there are occasional examples of the misuse of his name. Although Sarah, Abraham's wife, is not stated to have actually used the Lord's name, the fact that she "laughed" at what he said when he promised she would bear a son in a year's time may be regarded as a serious misuse of God's name: Genesis 18:10–15.

During the people's time in Egypt, although knowledge of God was limited and probably not developing, his name seems to have been known, especially after Moses returned from Midian with God's call to bring the people out of captivity. But their use of his name was not always of a reverent and believing nature. When Pharaoh added collecting straw to the brick-making and still expected the full quota of bricks, the Israelite foremen blamed Moses and used the Lord's name as a kind of curse:

> *May the Lord look upon you and judge you. You have made us a stench to Pharaoh and his officials have put a sword in their hand to kill us* (Ex. 5:21).

We even find the Lord's name coming out of the mouth of Pharaoh himself, though hardly in a reverent or believing spirit. When the plague of hail struck everything in his fields he says to Moses:

> *I have sinned...the Lord is righteous and I and my people are wrong. Pray to the Lord, for we have had enough thunder and hail* (Ex. 9:27–28).

When he first gives then retracts his permission to leave the land to worship the Lord, he uses a common blessing as a kind of curse:

> *The Lord be with you if I let you go along with your women and children!* (Ex. 10:10)

Eventually the people are released from Egypt through the "mighty hand of the Lord" which they find working for them and against the Egyptians, and soon after this "they cried out to the Lord," but the complaint they made to Moses shows how insincere their prayer was:

> *Was it because there were no graves in Egypt that you brought us to this desert to die?* (Ex. 14:10)

Further instances of the use of the Lord's name in a complaining spirit are: when they find themselves short of food and compare this with the abundance of food in Egypt (Ex. 16:2–3), and at Massah and Meribah when they were short of water and cried out "Is the Lord among us or not?" (Ex. 17:7).

If the story of Job dates from before Sinai, as seems likely, then it contains further instances of the abuse of God's name. When Job's children hold a party he gets up early and offers a sacrifice to God thinking, "Perhaps my children have sinned and cursed God in their hearts" (Job 1:5). For Job to say that, the cursing of God must have been a practice not altogether unknown. Shortly after this, when Job's body is struck, we find Job's wife advising him to "curse God and die" (Job 2:10). Although he refused to do this, it isn't long before he "opened his mouth and cursed the day of his birth," and the curse included the words "may God above not care about it" (Job 3:1–5).

It is true that none of these instances is idle swearing, which is what we tend to mean when we talk about "taking the Lord's name in vain," but they are surely just as wrong since they are uttered in a spirit which shows a complete lack of trust in God, love for him, or understanding of his goodness and faithfulness. They are therefore examples of what came to be forbidden under the third commandment.

The fourth commandment (Ex. 20:8–11) requires the seventh day or Sabbath to be kept holy, particularly by refraining from work. Separate consideration will be given to this commandment, but, since keeping the Sabbath holy was not practised until immediately before Sinai, we should hardly expect there to be instances of breaking it. It is sometimes said it was a creation ordinance, but if so there is no record of its being observed until Exodus 16 when the manna was given. Had Adam been guilty of failing to keep it after he left Eden? Had he failed to pass it on to the next generation? Or was it completely unknown until Moses told the people they must gather twice as much manna on the sixth day and none on the seventh, because it is "a day of rest, a holy Sabbath to the Lord" (Ex. 16:23)? The latter seems more likely, but this will be discussed in more detail in Chapter 9.

The fifth commandment (Ex. 20:12) requires us to honour our parents, that is, to respect and obey them. Ham, son of Noah, dishonoured his father when he "saw his father's nakedness and told his two brothers outside" (Gen. 9:22). They showed respect by covering Noah in such a way that they did not look on him. Lot's daughters did not respect their father when they made him drunk and induced him to lie with them (Gen. 19:30–35). Jacob can hardly be said to have respected his father Isaac when he lied to him in order to secure the blessing of the elder son (Gen. 27:19).

But Jacob himself suffered indignity at the hands of his eldest son Reuben who went and lay with his father's concubine Bilhah (Gen. 35:22), which Jacob remembered when he prophesied on his deathbed that Reuben "will no longer excel" (Gen. 49:4); he lost his birth right as the eldest son. Disrespect to parents was a sin from the beginning. Cain's murder of his brother Abel not only brought his parents grief over the loss of a son, but disappointment over their firstborn whose arrival had been greeted with such joy: "With the help of the Lord I have brought forth a man," said Eve (Gen. 4:1).

The sixth commandment against murder (Ex. 20:13) was also broken before it was declared. Cain's murder of Abel, his brother, has just been referred to (Gen. 4:8), which brought on him not only the Lord's rebuke but severe and lasting punishment. Later Lamech, a descendant of Cain, boasted of the murders he had committed (Gen. 4:23). No doubt the violence that preceded the Flood often led to murder (Gen. 6:9–13). After the Flood the commandment is anticipated by the law requiring capital punishment for murder (Gen. 9:6). Nevertheless, Simeon and Levi, Jacob's sons, committed mass murder in Shechem (Gen. 34:25–26). Moses himself, who was later to receive this law, killed an Egyptian (Ex. 2:11–12).

The seventh commandment (Ex. 20:14) condemns adultery, which carries with it other forms of sexual sin. Of this we find instances (as mentioned in Chapter 2) such as Lamech's bigamy (Gen. 4:19), Lot's daughters' incest (Gen. 19:30–38), Jacob's polygamy, and Reuben's intercourse with his father's concubine Bilhah (Gen. 35:22). Jacob's daughter Dinah was raped by Shechem, son of Hamor the Hivite, for which he paid a high price (Gen. 34). Judah lay with his daughter-in-law, Tamar, believing her to be a prostitute (Gen. 38:15). This shows that prostitution, an act which incurs sin on the man's as well as the woman's part, was practised in the ancient world and among the people of God. That homosexuality was practised before Sinai is illustrated by the men of Sodom (Gen. 19:4–5).

The eighth commandment against theft (Ex. 20:15) was broken by Rachel who "stole her father's household gods" (Gen. 31:19), but surely too by her father Laban who withheld Jacob's wages on a number of occasions (Gen. 31:5). Some would accuse Eve of theft for taking and eating the forbidden fruit.

The ninth commandment against "false witness" (Ex. 20:16) includes other forms of deceit, besides lying in court. Cain lied to God when he denied he knew the whereabouts of his brother Abel (Gen. 4:9). Abraham was guilty of misleading Pharaoh and later Abimelech, if not actually lying to them about Sarah (Gen. 12:11–13, 20:2), as did Isaac regarding Rebekah (Gen. 26:7). Rebekah and Jacob lied to Isaac (Gen. 27), Rachel deceived her father over his gods (Gen. 31:34–35) and Jacob's sons lied to Shechem and Hamor (Gen. 34:13–17), as they did to Jacob himself later over Joseph (Gen. 37:31–32).

The tenth commandment (Ex. 20:17) forbids covetousness, which was about the first sin ever committed—by Eve, when she

> ... *saw that the fruit of the tree was good for food and pleasing to the eye, and was desirable for gaining wisdom* (Gen. 3:6).

This last sin, since it concerns an inward feeling rather than an outward action, is at the bottom of other sins like murder, adultery and theft, examples of which have already been given. The first book and a half of the Bible is thus a catalogue of sins which afterwards became specified and codified at Sinai.

The Basis of the Detailed Laws to Follow

After the Lord had declared the Ten Commandments, he proceeded to "set before them" (Ex. 21:1) a whole catalogue of detailed laws which occupy a large part of the remaining books of Moses. These are by and large applications of the Ten Commandments to specific cases in the life of the people of Israel. They show how these great moral principles are worked out in that particular nation. They therefore require careful handling. On the one hand, they reflect the great eternal moral absolutes derived from the character of God himself and man, who is made in his image. On the other hand, they are adapted to the culture of a particular nation at a particular time in history. They are addressed to a people who have been "brought out of Egypt...the land of slavery" to inherit "the land the Lord your God is giving you" (Ex. 20:2, 12). So the literal details will apply only to the people of Israel during the old covenant period, although they will reflect some basic moral principles which are abiding.

The commandments were written on both sides of two stone tablets (Ex. 32:15–16). The usual explanation of this is that the first tablet contained the laws relating to God himself (I–IV) and the second those relating to other people (V–X). [See the Westminster Confession Chapter XIX.ii and the Westminster Larger Catechism Question 98.] Although this idea is convenient for theological purposes, it does not fit the practicalities so well, since the first four commandments are more than twice the length of the last six. An alternative view is that both tablets contained all ten commandments. Since they form a covenant, each party to it would have a copy so that the basis of the covenant between God and his people would be ever before them. This was the general practice with covenants in the ancient Near East.

> The customary division of the Decalogue into two tables stems from a misconception of the nature of the two tables, which were actually duplicates. (M.G. Kline)[25]

Nevertheless there is a distinction to be drawn between I–IV and V–X. This is brought out by Jesus who, when he was asked to give his view on which "of all the commandments…is the most important" (Mark 12:28), he declined to select any one of the Ten. Instead he quoted Deuteronomy 6:4–5:

> *Hear, O Israel, the Lord our God, the Lord, is one. Love the Lord your God with all your heart and with all your soul and with all your mind and with all your strength.*

But he did not leave it there, he added a second by quoting Leviticus 19:18:

> *Love your neighbour as yourself.*

The usual explanation of this is that his most important one summarised the first tablet and his second the second tablet. The first four commandments teach how to love the Lord your God and the last six how to love your neighbour (our duty to God and our duty to man). We may therefore

---

[25] Source unknown.

consider the detailed applications of the commandments from this perspective.

Love the Lord your God (I–IV)

The law sections of the rest of the Pentateuch refer much to God's demand for love and loyalty to him and his covenant. This is practised:

(a) by avoiding all compromise with heathen nations and their practices, particularly by making alliances with them or adopting their gods and forms of worship; this is the thrust of *the first two commandments*, to have no other gods and to refrain from idolatry;

(b) by following God's prescribed ways of worship.

In connection with (a) Exodus 22:20 says:

> *Whoever sacrifices to any god other than the Lord must be destroyed.*

Shortly after comes a long section (Ex. 23:10–31:17) which begins and ends with Sabbath regulations and in between contains instructions about the annual feasts (Ex. 23:14–19), which were in a sense held on Sabbath days, inasmuch as work was not allowed on them. This is followed by the promise of an angel to accompany them on their journey, whose commission is to keep them in God's ways by worshipping him alone and avoiding the gods of the nations whom he will drive out of Canaan (Ex. 23:23–33). Then comes a reaffirmation of the covenant whose book is sprinkled with blood, after which Moses is to go up the mountain and receive the tablets on which God had written the law he had declared by his voice (Ex. 24). Following this are the instructions about making the tabernacle and its furniture (Ex. 25–31).

But before Moses could return from the mountain and carry out these instructions, the incident of the golden calf occurs (Ex. 32) which causes Moses to break the stone tablets he is carrying down from the mountain. This signifies the breaking of the covenant with the Lord, who announces he is no longer personally with them in their journey (Ex. 33). So Moses has to obtain God's forgiveness and renew the covenant (Ex. 34) by receiving new stone tablets.

The Sabbath regulations are repeated (Ex. 35:1–5) before the construction of the tabernacle begins, which occupies the rest of Exodus. Leviticus 1–18 describes the duties of the priests and Levites, particularly in tabernacle worship. But this does not end the matter. Leviticus 19 is a collection of brief instructions, many of which are in commandment form, beginning "Do not..." and include references to the worship of God and its exclusivity: Leviticus 4–8, 26, 28–31. The chapter begins with the call to "be holy because the Lord your God is holy," and the words "I am the Lord" occur repeatedly.

There is more about heathen practices in Leviticus 20, along with punishments for breaking these rules. The book then returns to the duties of priests and Levites (Lev. 21–27) which are continued in Numbers as the journey from Sinai begins (Num. 3–10). The rest of Numbers contains more material of a ritual nature.

Deuteronomy, after the historical introduction, repeats the Ten Commandments (Deut. 5) and then proceeds to repeat the injunction to avoid all contact with heathen nations, apart from that involved in driving them out or destroying them (Deut. 7–13). There are further ritual regulations in Deuteronomy 14–18 about the difference between true and false worship.

However, Deuteronomy is also important for its stress on the inward as well as the outward. They are to know and keep the Lord's commands in order to love him (Deut. 6:1–9). It is in this passage that there occurs what Jesus later called "the first and great commandment," namely, to "love the Lord your God with all your heart and with all your soul and with all your strength" (Deut. 6:4, Mark 12:29). That this love does not mean sentimentality is made clear by the exhortation which follows to "fear the Lord your God, serve him only and take your oaths in his name" (Deut. 6:13). Love for God is not to be mere emotion, but a serious esteem for his greatness and goodness, and respect for his majesty. After God had rewritten the Commandments on new stone tablets and told Moses to "lead the people on their way," he gives an exhortation which is essentially spiritual: Deuteronomy 10:12–13. Shortly after this he tells them to "circumcise your hearts and do not be stiff-necked any longer" (Deut. 10:16). Deuteronomy 11 develops these ideas.

Deuteronomy ends with Moses' command to inscribe the words of the law on stones when they reach the Promised Land (Deut. 27:1–8). Half of them must stand on Mount Ebal to pronounce the curses of the law, and the other half on Mount Gerizim to pronounce its blessings (Deut. 27:9–28:68). Much of this, too, concerns loyalty to God and his worship. So it is no surprise that this is followed by the renewal of the covenant (Deut. 29). At the heart of this are the words

> *Make sure there is no man or woman, clan or tribe, among you today whose heart turns away from the Lord your God and worships the gods of these nations* (Deut. 29:18).

As Moses hands over the leadership to Joshua, he writes and reads the law to the people. During this the Lord himself appears at the tent in a pillar of cloud (Deut. 31:15) and warns Moses that

> *... these people will prostitute themselves to foreign gods and break the covenant I made with them* (Deut. 31:16).

Moses' final "blessing on the tribes" (Deut. 32–33) is on the basis that God's blessing rests on those who are faithful to him, otherwise they will receive only the curses.

All this shows that the first two commandments are first not just in order but importance. They are mostly about the respect for and obedience to God which constitute love. There is a sense, too, in which the next two commandments cannot be separated from the first two. Reverence for the "name of the Lord" is reverence for him. Offering worship to other gods and neglecting him is "misuse of his name." Likewise the *fourth commandment's* call to refrain from any work on the Sabbath day is primarily to enable his people to worship him. It is holy; separate to the Lord your God to recall how he created the earth in six days and rested on the seventh day. Clearly that does not mean that God was tired and needed a rest! The word *rest* or *Sabbath* means *cessation* rather than repose, and draws attention to the fact that God ceased from creating the universe not because he needed a rest but because he had finished his work as Creator. The Sabbath was blessed by God and made holy as an opportunity for his people to acknowledge him as Creator. If, during the days of the week they had been tempted to ascribe divinity to anything in the heavens and the earth, as the heathen did, the Sabbath would call them back to him as their Creator.

So on the whole the application of the third and fourth commandments to the detailed laws is interspersed with the application of the first two commandments. Nevertheless there are occasional reminders of the holiness of God's name in the development of the other laws, for example in Exodus 22:28:

> Do not blaspheme God or curse the ruler of your people.

Similarly in Leviticus 19:12:

Do not swear falsely in my name and so profane the name of your
God. I am the Lord.

However, the fourth commandment is nearly always referred to in the context of worship generally.

Love your neighbour (V–X)

If the first and great commandment concerns love and reverence for God, the second concerns love for neighbour. The second table of the law, commandments five to ten, spells this out. There is no orderly list of which specific laws apply to which particular commandments, for they appear somewhat haphazardly throughout the Pentateuch after Exodus 20.

The *fifth commandment* does not put in much of an appearance but there is half a verse in Leviticus 19:3:

Each of you must respect his father and mother.

There is also a passage about the punishment of a rebellious son in Deuteronomy 21:18–21.

The *sixth commandment* is given more space. Deuteronomy 19–21 may be seen as centring on this law. The "cities of refuge" passage in chapter 19 is clearly closely connected with killing, and allows exemption from punishment in the case of accidental homicide. A crime must be proved by witnesses (Deut. 19:15–21). The mention of killing raises the subject of war, which is dealt with in Deuteronomy 20. Deuteronomy 21 comes back to murder; in this case the killer is unknown and there is a danger that the whole community will bear the guilt. The regulations show how to deal with this situation. The law requiring capital punishment for murder includes instructions as to how to dispose of the body of the murderer in such a way as not to "desecrate the land the Lord your God is giving you" (Deut. 21:22). Rules about personal injuries in Deuteronomy 21:12–36 also come under this commandment; in fact this is the very first subject of the detailed laws and comes immediately after the commandments themselves.

The *seventh commandment* is applied in Leviticus 18, which goes into great detail about unlawful sexual relations, and in Deuteronomy 22:13–30 which has detailed laws on marriage violations. Deuteronomy 24:1–4 is the passage quoted by Jesus when he was questioned about divorce in Matthew 19.

The *eighth commandment* concerns the whole question of property and is dealt with in Exodus 22:1–15 and again in Deuteronomy 22:1–4. Failure to return property to its rightful owner is seen as a form of theft.

The *ninth commandment* raises the subject of true and false witness, and comes in after the "cities of refuge" law in Deuteronomy 19:15–22. For a serious crime, the witness of only one person is not sufficient.

The *tenth commandment* does not feature at all in the exposition of the Commandments. Other books will deal with that in great depth, notably the prophets and psalmists.

Just as there are hints of the first great commandment in the sins against the first table, so there are of the second table which is like it: love for neighbour. So these laws were not only about how the neighbour was **not** to be treated, but also about showing him love, mercy and kindness.

In Exodus 21:1–11 there are instructions about the treatment of servants. Servitude or slavery was permitted under the law, but there were rules. A servant had to be given the choice of freedom after seven years. Women had special safeguards. In the same chapter in which the second great commandment is first stated (Lev. 19:18) there is the instruction to farmers to consider the poor and needy when harvesting their crops; they must leave gleanings for them: Leviticus 19:9–10. Also, advantage was not to be taken of the vulnerability of the poor: Leviticus 19:13–18. Finally, the system of cities of refuge (Deut. 19) was intended for the protection of the innocent person who accidentally kills another and is thus open to the vengeance of the victim's relatives.

Thus, in one way or another, all these commandments on the second tablet show how the people of the old covenant were to love their neighbour. So what about the new covenant?

The Commandments in the Teaching of Jesus and the Apostles

Much more will need to be said on the whole question of the New Testament teaching on the law, but for the time being a brief summary of the approach of Jesus and his apostles to the Ten Commandments will round off this chapter. In the Sermon on the Mount Jesus stated he had not come to "abolish the law and the prophets but to fulfill them" (Matt. 5:17). This fulfilment is partly carried out in his own behaviour and partly in the way his teaching and that of his apostles filled out the scope of these laws.

Love the Lord your God (I–IV)

To fulfill the *first commandment* it is not enough to refrain from idolatry. From the time of their return from captivity the Jews were never again guilty of worshipping other gods. Indeed, they took their monotheism so far they were unable to entertain any idea of Jesus being Son of God, which was to them blasphemy. But Jesus brought out that God required more than nominal belief in his sole godhead—he seeks our hearts to "love the Lord your God with all your heart … soul … mind … and strength," which Jesus called "the first and great commandment" (Mark 12:29). He did not find this in the majority of the Jews, especially their leaders, and thus convicted them of breaking this law.

To fulfill the *second commandment* requires more than just not making graven images. We can form mental images of God, conceptions of him formed in the mind that fail to represent the truth about him. These may be codified in works of theology and ethics. When Jesus came the laws of Moses had been multiplied several times over in the Mishnah and Gemara, which contained the teachings of the rabbis over the centuries on how the laws of Moses were to be observed in every detail of life. God emerged as very strict, demanding attention to minute details of behaviour and giving no room for freedom. His pardon had to be bought by monetary offerings and animal sacrifices. Jesus brought a new image of God—as Father, who treats his children with love and can be prayed to accordingly: Luke 11:1–13. He receives sinners who come to him without gifts and sacrifices but utterly empty, as his parable of the lost son beautifully illustrates: Luke 15:11–32. The apostle John took up this teaching in his first letter when he taught that "God is love" (1 Jn. 4:16). His final words, which some think were the last words of the whole New Testament, were "Little children, keep yourselves from idols" (1 Jn. 5:21). In the context of the letter it is unlikely John was referring to graven images; more likely he spoke of concepts of God which developed when Christ's gospel met Greek philosophy and produced Gnosticism, which John exposes in his letter.

Jesus also widened the scope of the *third commandment* to include misuse of all words, not only the name of the Lord but even careless ones. These proceed from the heart and reveal whether it is good or corrupt. For this reason men will have to account for every careless word they have spoken. On this evidence they are acquitted or condemned (Matt. 12:33–37). Worst of all, said Jesus, is not misuse of the name of the Lord or even his own name (Son of Man) but blasphemy or speaking against the Holy Spirit, which is unforgivable (Matt. 12:31–32).

On the *fourth commandment* Jesus did not support the excessively rigorous rules which the rabbis had added to the Mosaic Law. He healed on the Sabbath, told a man healed to carry his mattress and walk away, allowed his disciples to pluck ears of corn, and so on. His apostles developed this teaching by advocating the position that one day was no more special than another, but that all days should be lived to the honour and glory of Christ and the Father (Rom. 14:5–8, Gal. 4:10, Col. 2:16–17). The teaching in the last passage about the Sabbath being a shadow of things to come is developed by the writer of Hebrews, who may have been an ex-rabbi, since he argues like one. For a person to observe the Sabbath in gospel days means to rest from his own work and enter into that rest, that is, the rest of faith (Heb. 4:1–12). A fuller explanation of this point will be given in Chapter 9.

Love your neighbour (V–X)

Luke 2:51 shows Jesus personally and literally observing the fifth commandment and obeying his parents. This was also the teaching of Paul in Ephesians 6:1–3 and Colossians 3:20. He also applied this teaching more widely to the domestic sphere by instructing slaves to submit to their masters: Ephesians 6:5–8, Colossians 3:22–25. Peter's teaching is similar in 1 Peter 2:18–25. The submissiveness of wives to husbands is also taught by Paul in Ephesians 5:22–24 and Colossians 3:18, and by Peter in 1 Peter 3:1–8. Since the church is a kind of family the principle applies there too. Members are to "respect those who are over you in the Lord" (1 Thes. 5:12) and even to "obey… and submit to their authority" (Heb. 13:17). All Christians are to "submit to one another out of reverence for Christ" (Eph. 5:21).

Furthermore, those who are recipients of this respect and obedience are to be worthy of it by fulfilling their responsibilities to those from whom they expect respect. Fathers are told: "do not exasperate your children but bring them up in the training and instruction of the Lord" (Eph. 6:4, cf. Col. 3:21). Husbands are told: "love your wives, just as Christ loved the church" (Eph. 5:28–33, cf. Col. 3:19, 1 Pet. 3:7). Masters are told to treat slaves "in the same way," that is, as serving Christ and therefore not to ill-treat them (Eph. 6:9).

There seems to be a principle of submission to authority running through the ethical teaching of the New Testament. This was a live issue in those times, when the Jews were ruled by the Romans. But Jesus recognised their authority, which could be acknowledged without lessening that of God's: Matthew 22:15–22. Indeed, obedience to legitimate authority was part of obedience to God. Paul taught that, since "the authorities that exist have been established by God," to disobey them is to disobey him: Romans 13:1–7, 1 Peter 2:13–15. But Jesus' principle of giving God what is God's is shown, not so much in the apostolic teaching as in its practice. The apostles had to make difficult choices in Acts 4:19–20. Their refusal to obey seems only to have applied where the authorities required their disobedience to God. Rebellion is not encouraged, even against bad rulers (Rom. 13:2, which was written during the reign of Nero). Wicked rulers are to be left to God, who will deal severely with them, as the book of Revelation shows: Revelation 17–18.

Jesus considered the *sixth commandment* in the Sermon on the Mount and extended it to feelings of anger which give vent to insulting language and quarrelling: Matthew 5:21–26, and to non-retaliation in Matthew 5:38–41. Jesus practised what he preached and only expressed anger and indulged violence where God himself was being dishonoured, not where the matter was purely personal, when he showed great forbearance, as Peter wrote in 1 Peter 2:23–25. Paul also called for forbearance in disputes in Romans 12:19–21.

Jesus also gave his interpretation of the *seventh commandment* in the Sermon and the Mount, but, as with murder, extended it to inner feelings, in this case to the lust which creates sexual fantasies. This must be firmly controlled: Matthew 5:27–30. To this he added some words on divorce: Matthew 5:31–32 (further developed in Matt. 19:1–12). The current practice was to divorce for any and every reason which would include dislike of a wife and preference for another woman. But Jesus confined it to a clear breach of marriage vows. The apostle Paul applied the principle to the Gentile world and dealt especially with the case of the breakdown of a relationship between a Christian and a non-Christian: 1 Corinthians 7.

On the *eighth commandment* Jesus and the apostles certainly upheld the duty of honesty in all things. For example, Paul, in exhorting the Christians of Ephesus, ordered all Christians to cease living like Gentiles and to live worthily of the name of Christ, specifically stating:

> … *he who has been stealing must steal no longer…*

But he does not leave it at that, he states the positive alternative, that of working in order to share with the poor:

> …*but must work, doing something useful with his own hands, that he may have something to share with those in need* (Eph. 4:28).

Jesus condemned the Pharisees and Scribes because they devour widows' houses, which presumably means they turned them out of their houses in order to possess them themselves: Mark 12:40. Interestingly, Mark immediately goes on to speak of a widow who "out of her poverty put everything into the treasury" (Mark 12:44–49). This suggests that this commandment should include not merely negative restraint from theft and dishonesty, but practising generosity. Paul has some very extensive teaching on giving in 2 Corinthians 8–9.

The *ninth commandment* on false witness is probably the one in view in Jesus' words on oath-taking in Matthew 5:33–37, although it could also apply to making oaths to the Lord and come under the third commandment. It is all about speaking the truth, about words which can be trusted, whether uttered in court (which appears to have been the background of the original commandment) or spoken in ordinary conversation. Paul is also strong on truth-speaking in Ephesians 4:25, on the ground that trustworthiness is the basis of living in society—"for we are all members of one body"—which would seem to refer here, not just to the church but the body politic. Most transactions are carried out in words, and where words cannot be trusted society breaks down.

In connection with the *tenth commandment*, Jesus spoke strongly against covetousness, which he said came from within, from an unclean spirit, along with things like murder, theft and adultery; indeed covetousness is the root cause of them: Mark 7:20–23. When a brother came to Jesus about a disputed inheritance, Jesus saw that the motive was not really need or justice but greed, and told him and the crowd to "be on guard against all kinds of greed" (Luke 12:13–15). The apostles included covetousness in their lists of sins or "works of the flesh" (Rom. 1:29, Eph. 3:3, Col. 3:5).

So it becomes clear that what Jesus and the apostles were doing was getting behind the laws of Moses to the eternal moral absolutes which cover feelings, motives and words as well as actions. The fact that Jesus and the apostles frequently quoted the Ten Commandments or other passages from the Sinai law does not mean they give it the same place as the people of the old covenant did. The parts they quoted are those that reflect the eternal moral absolutes that predate Sinai. In fact they were going back beyond the fall itself to a time when man's relationship with God was based on love and trust and needed no spoken or written law. This comes out most, of course, in Jesus' great summary of the law as love to God and neighbour (Mark 12:29–31). When Paul quotes the commandments he tends to do so in the context of their fulfilment in Christ and of the spirit of love (e.g., Rom. 13:8–10, Eph. 6:2). The law itself could only make people externally righteous, it could not make them love God or each other. This required Christ's redemptive work, which did achieve it, as Paul said in Romans 8:3–4:

> *What the law was powerless to do in that it was weakened by the sinful nature, God did in sending his own Son in the likeness of sinful man to be a sin offering. And so he condemned sin in sinful man, in order that the righteous requirements of the law might be fully met in us, who do not live according to the sinful nature but according to the Spirit.*

The code of Sinai was only fully workable in a theocratic society, where all accepted it as the basis of behaviour, and where there were authorities to enforce it. But Christ and the New Testament show how it can be adapted for believers throughout the world.

CHAPTER 5
THE PURPOSE OF THE LAW

From the time it was revealed at Mount Sinai the Law played a prominent part in the life of the people of God. The details take up much of the remaining books of Moses, and there are frequent references in the histories, the psalms and the prophets. What was the purpose of it all? Is it possible to find a simple statement which sums it all up? As it happens, this is possible, but it lies in the New Testament rather than the Old. Paul's successful visit to the towns of the Roman province of Galatia was quickly followed by that of certain Jewish believers from Jerusalem who tried to persuade these Gentile believers to be circumcised and to keep other laws of Moses, such as the observance of special days. Paul had to write and tell them that this was unnecessary, in fact if they did so it would detract from their faith in Christ and his cross, which would be rendered virtually ineffective for them (Gal. 5:1–4).

He took up this matter again in his letter to the Romans. Of the several passages where he speaks of the Law the most relevant for our purpose here is

> *The law was added so that the trespass might increase* (Rom. 5:20).

The Sinai law is a prominent theme in the Old Testament and occupies much of its contents. So if it is now null and void what use had it ever been? This was a question raised by both Jews and Gentiles. Paul answers this very succinctly in Galatians 3:19:

> *What then was the purpose of the law? It was added because of transgressions until the seed to whom the promise referred had come.*

This and Romans 5:20 tell us three things about the
purpose of the Law.

1. It was added to the promise, that is, to the covenant
God made with Abraham. Strictly speaking the word
translated *added* in Romans 5:20 is not the word used in
Galatians 3:19, but a variant of the word used in Romans
5:12 translated *entered*. Sin was not in the world originally, it
entered or *came in* (ESV) later. Similarly the Law (of Sinai)
was not in the world at the beginning, but *entered* (Rom.
5:20). Here the word has a prefix—*PARA*—which means
alongside, that is, alongside sin. Sin came in and Law came in
alongside it, because of the breaking of law by sin. It was
added. But why?

2. It was "because of transgressions" (Gal. 3:19) or
"trespass" (Rom. 5:20). Sin was the reason for law. What
does this mean?

a. It means that the law gives knowledge of sin; it
defines and exposes it:

Every one who sins breaks the law, in fact, sin is lawlessness (1
Jn. 3:4).

As Paul said

I would not have known what sin was except through the law
(Rom. 7:7).

b. It makes us feel the seriousness of sin: Through the
law we become conscious of sin (Rom. 3:20). The more we
know of the law the more we see sin's vileness. This is
what Paul means in Romans 5:20 when he says, "so that
the trespass might increase," that is, increase our sense of
sin's heinousness. We feel how foreign it is to God, how
much he hates it. "Sin becomes utterly sinful" (Rom. 7:13).
Far from preventing sin, it even provokes us to sin more:
it "seizes the opportunity afforded by the commandment
to produce every kind of covetous desire" (Rom. 7:8, 11,

13). It tells us of sins we were not even aware of, and lures us to commit them. This is probably why he refers to the law as "the power of sin" (1 Cor. 15:56).

c. It makes us feel sin's power. Sin has us in a vicelike grip from which we cannot get free. This was Paul's experience when under conviction of sin: "I am sold as a slave to sin" (Rom. 7:14). It controls us (Rom. 7:5); it dominates us; we are bound to it as a wife to her husband (Rom. 7:2). The more he tried to stop sinning and start doing righteousness, the less he succeeded: Romans 7:15–16. He had to conclude that "sin lives in me" (Rom. 7:17). This was what the law was doing to him: it was urging him not to righteousness, but to sin. The more he knew of the law the more he wanted to break it. It creates division in the personality (Rom. 7:15–23, 25b). All the time we are breaking the law with one part of us, we are agreeing with it in another part. No wonder he called himself "a wretched man" (Rom. 7:24) and, once he had found salvation in Christ, no wonder he was so thankful (Rom. 7:25).

3. It was to be in operation "until the seed to whom the promise referred had come" (Gal. 3:19), that is, until the promised Messiah arrived. From all this we can deduce what the Law's purpose was. During the time of its operation, the Law performed many useful functions. It even has purposes for believers in Christ during the period of his kingdom.

A. Its purpose for Israel

(1) It defined the covenant relationship between God and his people.

God had promised to make a special people from Abraham and to give them their own land:

I will make you into a great nation and I will bless you; I will make your name great and you will be a blessing. I will bless those who bless you, and whoever curses you I will curse; and all peoples of the earth will be blessed through you (Gen. 12:1–3).

The whole land of Canaan where you are now an alien I will give you as an everlasting possession to you and your descendants after you; and I will be their God (Gen. 17:8).

But this promise imposed certain demands on them: they must "keep my covenant" (Gen. 19:9). To Abraham at the time this meant that he and his descendants must be circumcised, as a sign that they were God's and undertook to fulfill their obligations to him. Few of these were spelled out until the nation reached Mount Sinai when the whole code of law was revealed.

At Sinai God first reaffirmed the covenant promise:

Now if you obey me fully and keep my covenant, then out of all nations you will be my treasured possession. Although the whole earth is mine you will be for me a kingdom of priests and a holy nation (Ex. 19:5–6).

God then added his laws, which were thus part of the covenant. God's part was to make and keep the promise; their part was to keep the laws attached to it. Like Abraham they had to "keep my covenant." The people agreed to this, even before they heard what the laws were!

The people all responded together, "We will do everything the Lord has said" (Ex. 19:8).

Thereafter the Law is frequently referred to as a covenant. For example:

He declared to you his covenant, the Ten Commandments (Deut. 4:13).

The preface to the Commandments and thus to the whole law contains the words

The Lord our God made a covenant with us in Horeb (Deut. 5:2).

At the end of the recital of the Commandments, it is said that their obedience to these laws will guarantee the enjoyment of the promises:

> So be careful to do what the Lord your God has commanded you to do; do not turn aside to the right or to the left. Walk in all the ways that the Lord your God has commanded you, so that you may live and prosper and prolong your days in the land that you will possess (Deut. 5:32–33).

When the agreement is ratified at a special ceremony, it is said to be "sealed with the blood of the covenant" (Ex. 24:8). The law of the Sabbath is singled out as a special covenant sign:

> The Israelites are to observe the Sabbath, celebrating it for the generations to come as a lasting covenant. It will be a sign between me and the Israelites for ever (Ex. 31:16–17).

After he had recited the whole Law to the generation which was about to take possession of the promised land, Moses instructed them to hold what can only be described as a covenant ceremony as soon as they were all safely across the river Jordan. The tribes were to divide into two groups, one standing on Mount Ebal and the other on Mount Gerizim so that one group could proclaim the curses of the covenant and the other its blessings (Deut. 27–28). This instruction is followed by the words

> These are the terms of the covenant the Lord commanded Moses to make with the Israelites in Moab (Deut. 29:1).

There are more references to the covenant in the rest of that chapter. Therefore to break any of the laws was to break the covenant. Not to be circumcised was to risk being cut off from the people, which was probably why God threatened to kill Moses for not circumcising his son (Ex. 4:24–26). Worshipping idols was breaking the covenant and risked "many disasters and difficulties" (Deut. 31:16, 20–21). To bring foreigners who were uncircumcised into the temple was to break the covenant (Ezek. 44:7), as it was to break the Sabbath, which could even incur the death penalty (Ex. 31:15–16). Even breach of the marriage laws was breach of the covenant (Mal. 2:10–12).

The trouble that the people frequently had with the surrounding nations is usually connected with their failure to keep the law of the Lord. For example, the war between Rehoboam, king of Judah, and Shishak, king of Egypt is attributed to their disobedience:

> *After Rehoboam's position as king was established and he had become strong, he and all Israel with him abandoned the law of the Lord. Because they had been unfaithful to the Lord, Shishak king of Egypt attacked Jerusalem in the fifth year of king Rehoboam* (2 Chr. 12:1–2).

Centuries later, when the ten northern tribes (Israel or Ephraim) are sent into exile, the reason given is their breach of the covenant of Sinai by flouting its laws:

> *When the Lord made a covenant with the Israelites, he commanded them: "Do not worship any other gods or bow down to them (the first commandment)…You must always be careful to keep the decrees and ordinances, the laws and commands he wrote for you"* (2 Kgs. 17:34–41).

In the teaching of the prophets too, breaking the laws is breaking the covenant with God, for example:

> *Listen to the terms of the covenant and declare them to the people of Judah and to those who live in Jerusalem. Tell them that this is what the Lord, the God of Israel, says: "Cursed is the man who does not obey the terms of this covenant—the terms I commanded your forefathers when I brought them out of Egypt"* (Jer. 11:1–8).

A similar passage is Ezekiel 20. The Psalms too equate the covenant with the Law:

> *To the wicked God says, "What right have you to take my covenant on your lips? You hate my instruction and cast my words behind you"* (Psalm 18:16–17).

...*they did not keep God's covenant, and refused to abide by his law* (Psalm 78:10).

(2) It restrained sin in the nation

This is what the Reformers called the *usus politicus*, which they apply to the world generally in spite of its ignorance of a large part of the law.[26] Calvin wrote:

> The second function of the law is this: at least by fear of punishment to restrain certain men who are untouched by any care for what is just and right unless compelled by hearing the dire threats of the law.[27]

As already mentioned, the people of Israel, although holy or separated to the Lord, were still sinners. When they committed sin God was displeased, for they were not living according to their status as the people of a holy God. God acted therefore to restrain their sin in a number of ways. As Paul says in Galatians 3:19 "the law was added because of transgressions." In Romans 5:20 Paul wrote "the law was added so that the trespass may increase." Sin is not confined to the act of the one man, Adam, which is "the trespass" he is referring to here (Rom. 5:15, 17, 18). Sin is committed by everyone in all sorts of ways. The law of Moses revealed how widespread it was.

(a) *He wrote it into their national constitution.* All nations have some kind of law-code, but in most cases this is confined to crimes rather than sins, that is, to offences either against other persons or against the state. In the case of Israel, however, the law-code spelled out, in addition to crimes, sins against God himself, even those which had little direct effect on other people, such as worshipping other gods or breaking the Sabbath.

---

[26] E.F. Kevan, *The Grace of Law*, 38.

[27] Calvin, *Institutes*, II.vii.10.

(b) *He threatened punishments for the non-observance of his laws.* In the law we sometimes find punishments to be inflicted by Israel's judges for crimes committed against other people. But in addition we find punishments threatened by God himself, which were impossible for men to execute, such as sending diseases among them or raising up war against them. For example, in 2 Samuel 6:7 a man dropped dead by the hand of God for infringing what seemed a minor detail, which could harm no one else—touching the ark of the covenant. In other cases large numbers of people were affected by sins against God. Several times in the period of the judges apostasy from God brought invading armies or bands against them. For example, the people

forsook the Lord...and worshipped various gods of the people around them. They provoked the Lord to anger... (and) he handed them over to raiders who plundered them (Judg. 2:13–14).

This can be multiplied many times in Israel's history.

(c) *He raised up prophets,* whose ministry was largely to remind the people of their covenant relationship with God, to point out how they were breaking it, to remonstrate with them in order to get them to repent and, if this was not forthcoming, to threaten them with God's punishments. On occasions they had to point out that the troubles they were already suffering were God's punishments. For example

Ah, sinful nation, a people loaded with guilt, a brood of evildoers, children given to corruption! They have forsaken the Lord, they have spurned the Holy One of Israel and turned their backs on him. Why should you be beaten any more? Why do you persist in rebellion? Your whole head is injured, your whole heart afflicted... Your country is desolate, your cities burned with fire, your fields are being stripped by foreigners right before you... (Isa. 1:4–7).

This message was the largest part of the ministry of all the 'writing' prophets. It shows what Paul meant when he spoke of the Law as being "added because of transgressions." It also explains his further words

> Before this faith came, we were held prisoners by the law, locked up until faith should be revealed. So the law was put in charge... (Gal. 3:23–24).

The law acted as a supervisor (Gal. 3:25) or custodian, the *paidagōgos* of Roman society—a servant whose job was to discipline and keep the children of the family in order on behalf of the father. The law was the servant of Israel's 'Father' to promote good behaviour and restrain bad behaviour.

> The Mosaic administration, as a legal administration, was related to Israel as little children who did not quite understand the greatness and goodness of God's grace.[28]

Calvin wrote:

> Paul's statement appears to be very true: that the Jews were kept under the charge of a tutor (Gal. 3:24) until the seed should come for whose sake the promise had been given. For since they had not come to know Christ intimately, they were like children whose weakness could not bear the full knowledge of heavenly things.[29]

On the *paidagōgos* see also pages 118 and 129, on Galatians 3:23–24.

(3) It foreshadowed the gospel

Paul said that this state of things would continue "until the seed to whom the promise referred had come" (Gal. 3:19). Most of us are aware that the Old Testament contains types of Christ and the gospel, that is, figures which represent certain aspects of the person and work of Christ.

---

[28] W.A. van Gemeren, *Five Views of Law and Gospel*, 29.

[29] *Institutes* II.vii.2.

These usually appear in individuals like Moses or David, or certain events in Israel's history such as the flood or the Exodus, or in prophecies, some of which are quoted in the New Testament.

However, the law too plays its part. It has been described as "the womb from which the gospel is born." When Paul confronted the Judaizers in Colosse who were seeking to impose the Mosaic laws on these largely Gentile Christians, he described these laws as "a shadow of things that were to come; the reality, however, is found in Christ" (Col. 2:16–17). When the sun is behind a person approaching, his shadow appears first. The shadow bears a very primitive resemblance to the person; the shape is clear but not the details of his appearance. The Old Testament laws are like a shadow compared with Christ himself. They reveal in advance something of his shape, but do not give the full picture.

The letter to the Hebrews also speaks of the ministry of priests under the law as a "copy and shadow of what is in heaven" (Heb. 8:5). The idea of shadow and substance show both continuity and discontinuity. It was the same God who spoke both the old and the new; he spoke in old times (Heb. 1:1) and now speaks in Christ. More generally, Hebrews 10:1 states "the law is only a shadow of the good things that are coming, not the realities themselves." Although these references are mainly to the ritual aspects of the law, the same principle applies to other parts. Put together, the laws paint a picture of a perfect man. No human being ever attained to this, no one ever perfectly obeyed the whole law (James 3:1–2). The perfect man is Christ who was to come, whose perfection is foreshadowed in the law which he kept perfectly. But even this was only a shadow, for his character and behaviour went far beyond the externals which comprise the law of Moses. His heart too, his feelings, motives and attitudes, were perfect. The law was thus a shadow of a perfect man, but the reality did not appear until he did.

Of what use was this to the people of Israel? It could give them an ideal to long after. All around them was disobedience to the law and even the best were not perfect. In Galatians 3:10 Paul quotes Deuteronomy 27:26:

> *Cursed is everyone who does not continue in the Book of the Law*

and James writes

> *... whoever keeps the whole law and yet stumbles at just one point is guilty of breaking all of it* (James 2:10).

This condemns every Israelite of being guilty and cursed. This is why Paul in writing of the Jew in Romans 3:10 says:

> *There is no one righteous, not even one; ...*

After quoting several passages which specify certain sins of the Jews, he draws his conclusion in verses 19–20:

> *Now we know that whatever the law says, it says to those who are under the law, so that every mouth may be silenced and the whole world held accountable to God. Therefore no one will be held righteous in his sight by observing the law; rather, through the law we become conscious of sin* (Rom. 3:19–20).

The law he has quoted was given to Israel, it is they who are under the law. They knew it and consented to it, so that they had no excuse. The mouth of every Jew was silenced by their knowledge of and consent to the law. It held them accountable. It was therefore, no use their appealing to their possession or knowledge of the law for righteousness in the sight of God. All they could get from it was a consciousness of sin. If it is asked why he brings the whole world into this, it is because this is his conclusion from the whole passage beginning in Romans 1:18. He has already convicted the Gentiles that they are "without excuse" (Rom. 1:20). From Romans 2 he turned to the Jews to convict them similarly.

The Bible records the character flaws and behaviour errors of its greatest personalities: Abraham, Noah, David and so on. Would there ever be one who will keep the Law perfectly, one who was not "guilty" and "cursed," one who was an exception to the statement that "there is not even one righteous person," who will be qualified to bring about the promised redemption? Such a one had been promised, and merely to believe in his coming and to long for it was sufficient for salvation in those times. This faith was expressed in performing the sacrifices through the appointed priests. To do this counted for righteousness.

Best of all was to believe the original promise of Genesis 3:15, which had been transmitted to them by the very one through whom they received the Law—Moses. This promise was repeated and enlarged on by the writing prophets and the psalmists. So, though the Israelite could not come to Christ in the way the New Testament believer can, he could believe the promise of Christ as enshrined in the history, ritual law, and prophecy and be saved. Abraham believed in God's promise of a son and "he (God) credited it to him as righteousness" (Gen. 15:6). So those who could see, however dimly, that there was more to these laws than instructions and that they pointed to one to come who would perfectly keep them could also be counted righteous. The situation of the believer under the old covenant is comparable to that of a child to whom a rich legacy is left, but which he cannot use until he comes of age. The money is promised to him though he cannot enjoy it. What he can do, however, is to believe it is his and rejoice in the expectation of it. So the Israelite could not enjoy what believers in Christ enjoy, but they could believe it and count it as theirs in anticipation.

Its purpose for Christians

The duration of the Law's function as a supervisor was limited; it was only "until the seed to whom the promise referred had come" (Gal. 3:19). This was the promised Messiah, Jesus Christ. What purpose does the Law serve now that he has come, or in other words, what is its purpose for Christians?

(1) It prefigures Christ

This is the first thing Christians need to know about the Law. They have the substance of what to Israel was only the shadow. They have come of age and enjoy the reality of what was only promised to Israel. After his resurrection, Jesus sought to persuade his disciples that his death had not been a mistake, but was in fact the main purpose of his life on earth. We are told how, when he overtook two of them as they were returning to Emmaus,

> ... beginning with Moses and all the prophets, he explained to them what was said in all the Scriptures concerning himself (Luke 24:27).

Later he told the whole company

> Everything must be fulfilled that is written of me in the Law of Moses, the Prophets and the Psalms (Luke 24:44).

Most of us are familiar with certain passages in the prophets and the Psalms which foretell his life, ministry and sufferings, such as Isaiah 11 and 53, Psalm 51 and 110. But how does the Law of Moses prefigure him?

He himself frequently made the claim that his whole life on the earth was lived in obedience to the Father:

> I seek not to please myself but him who sent me (John 5:30).

> I do always what pleases him (John 8:29).

> This command [to lay down his life] I received from my Father (John 10:18).

... the Father who sent me commanded me what to say and how to say it... whatever I say is just what the Father has told me to say (John 12:49–50).

I have obeyed my Father's commandments and remain in his love (John 15:10).

He had "come to do God's will" (Heb. 10:7) and to be obedient to him (Philip. 2:9). This meant more than obeying the Law of Moses but it certainly included that, as can be proved from the accounts in the Gospels of his life. This can be studied under the two headings of his active obedience (what he did) and his passive obedience (what was done to him).

(a) His Active Obedience

Paul wrote that Jesus was "born under law" (Gal. 4:4), that is, born during the old covenant period with obligations to observe the requirements of that covenant. Although he had come to bring in a new covenant, he himself was committed to the old one, the law. There is a sense in which Jesus as a man was more a Jew than a Christian! He did not, as a man, have the freedom from the Law that he was to bestow on his followers. So we find that from the very beginning of his life on earth he scrupulously kept the Mosaic regulations. He was circumcised on the eighth day and "named Jesus, the name the angel had given him before he was conceived" (Luke 2:21). Later,

> *When the time of their purification according to the Law of Moses had been accomplished, Joseph and Mary took him to Jerusalem to present him to the Lord, (as it is written in the Law of the Lord, "every firstborn male is to be consecrated to the Lord"), and to offer a sacrifice in keeping with what is said in the Law of the Lord: "a pair of doves or two young pigeons"* (Luke 2:22–24).

We are told that it was only

> *When Joseph and Mary had done everything required by the Law of the Lord, they returned to Galilee ...* (Luke 2:39).

As he grew up Jesus was careful to keep the fifth commandment: after his *Bar-mitzvah* at the age of thirteen,

> ... *he went down to Nazareth with them* [his parents] *and was obedient to them* (Luke 2:51).

As well as attending the Passover (Luke 2:41–42) he also attended the synagogue on the Sabbath day (Luke 4:16), although he was frequently charged with breaking the Sabbath (John 5:19, 9:16). Evidently he wore tassels on his cloak (Luke 8:40) as required by Numbers 15:38–40. He was careful to keep his special works of healing within the Law. Leprosy was strictly regulated under the Law and a healed leper had to be pronounced clean by a priest before being accepted back into society. Jesus obeyed this law: Luke 5:14, 17:14.

He made frequent appeals to the law when appropriate. When asked about eternal life by an expert in the law and a (synagogue?) ruler, he referred them to the Law (Luke 10:26, 18:20). When in dispute with the Pharisees about his authority to heal and teach, he claimed to be in conformity with the Law, saying "Do not think I will accuse you before the Father. Your accuser is Moses, on whom your hopes are set" (John 5:45). When accused of relying on his own testimony he again appealed to the Law:

> *In your own law it is written that the testimony of two men is valid. I am one who testifies for myself; my other witness is the Father who sent me* (John 8:17).

Not only did he observe the Law in every particular, but he went beyond this and brought out the *spirit of the Law* more than anyone had ever done. His Sermon on the Mount is the most obvious as well as the best example of this, showing how God requires more than a mere outward adherence to the Law's commands. As well as this, he proved that his Sabbath healings, while they involved some work on his part and that of the patient, were in keeping with the Law's requirement of showing mercy and kindness (Luke 13:10–17, 14:1–6). He condemned the Pharisees and rabbis because, while they were stringent in what they demanded both of themselves and others, they did absolutely nothing to help anyone carry out these demands (Luke 11:46).

In short, he was the perfect Jew. If, as the Psalmist said, "the law of the Lord is perfect" (Psalm 19:7), then one who obeys it perfectly is a perfect man. In his teaching on the Law in Matthew 5 he stated that he had not "come to abolish but fulfill the law" (Matt. 5:17) Nothing in the law "will by any means disappear until everything is accomplished" (Matt. 5:18). "Fulfill" and "accomplish" is exactly what he did, as has been shown in his perfect obedience to it. So Paul wrote that "Christ is the end of the law" (Rom. 10:4), the *telos*, the goal at which it was aiming, but never reached because of human weakness and depravity.

> For what the law was powerless to do in that it was weakened by the sinful nature, God did by sending his own Son in the likeness of sinful man to be a sin offering. …in order that the righteous requirements of the law might be fully met in us, who do not live according to the sinful nature but according to the Spirit. (Rom. 8:3–4).

In order to do this he had to do more than live a perfectly law-abiding life. He had to become "a sin offering" (Rom. 8:3). Although he was born and lived under the law, the old covenant, yet he came to bring in a new covenant, and he anticipated this in his life and teaching. He did this from the beginning, for when he came to be baptised by John in spite of having nothing of which to repent, he justified his action by claiming it was to "fulfill all righteousness" (Matt. 3:15). Perhaps the emphasis there is on *all*; he fulfilled not only the righteousness of the old covenant but of the new, for which baptism, which was not required under the Law, was to be the way of entry into the kingdom he had come to set up. But to bring this about he had to do more than obey God ACTIVELY, he had also to obey him PASSIVELY.

(b) His Passive Obedience

Christ became "obedient to death" (Philip. 2:8), which was the ultimate purpose of his mission. He was "born under law to redeem those under law" (Gal. 4:4–5). The Law contained not only precepts but punishments; there were blessings for obedience but curses for disobedience (Deut. 28). The ultimate curse was death under the wrath of God, which Christ endured in the three hours of darkness which descended on Jerusalem at midday when he had been hanging on the cross for three hours, after which he cried out

My God, my God, why have you forsaken me? (Matt. 27:46)

Death is ultimately separation from God, which is what he experienced in the three hours' darkness. That his death was under the curse of God not merely the sentence of man is demonstrated in his being hung on a cross or tree, for the Law states

anyone who is hung on a tree is under God's curse (Deut. 21:23).

Paul used this to prove that

Christ redeemed us from the curse of the law by becoming a curse for us,... (Gal. 3:13).

This was **prefigured** in the ceremonies and sacrifices required under the Law. In Colossians 2:17 Paul describes these as

... a shadow of things that were to come; the reality, however, is found in Christ.

Hebrews 9:9 uses the word *illustrations*; Hebrews 9:23 uses the word *copies,* and Hebrews 10:1 also calls them a *shadow.* Hebrews 9 shows how these old sacrifices pointed towards Christ's passive obedience. What was done to bulls and goats was done to him (Heb. 9:12–13). This was why he had to shed blood. No other form of death would fill the bill.

So Christ was not just the victim but the priest who offered the sacrifice. It was "when he came as high priest of the good things that are already here" (or "are to come," NIV mg) in order to enter the "more perfect tabernacle" that he had to shed "his own blood" and by it "enter the Most Holy Place once for all" (Heb. 9:11–12). In this way he fulfilled in himself the ultimate purposes of the Law.

- He gained entrance into the very presence of God on our behalf:

  For Christ did not enter into a man-made sanctuary that was only a copy of the true one; he entered into heaven itself now to appear for us in God's presence (Heb. 9:24).

- In order that we may be acceptable in God's presence he

  ... cleanse[d] *our consciences from acts that lead to death, so that we may serve the living God* (Heb. 9:14).

- In this way he replaced the old covenant with a new one: "he is the mediator of a new covenant." By this covenant, sins which could not be forgiven under the old covenant were not merely forgiven (Heb. 9:15) but erased from the divine memory (Heb. 10:17). This brought to an end the entire sacrificial system (Heb. 10:18).

It is a great means of assurance to Christians to know that the one they call their Saviour did not come out of the blue, but was promised long before. In fact it is not too much to say that the nation of Israel was raised up at least partly to safeguard and transmit the ancient promise, first given at the fall in Genesis 3:15, which is about the one who will come to redeem fallen humanity. In fact the whole organisation of Israel was geared toward showing what he will be like and what he will do.

This teaching also had an important place in the proclamation of the gospel, particularly to Jews, who needed convincing that Jesus was truly the promised Messiah. So we find the apostles doing what Jesus did with his disciples after the resurrection—showing them from Scripture the way he fulfilled both the Law and the Prophets. Peter did this at the Feast of Pentecost when Jews from all over the empire were gathered in Jerusalem, as did Paul when he made a point of beginning in the synagogue if there was one in the towns he evangelised, where we find him reasoning with the Jews and seeking to persuade them that Jesus is the Christ. Even when a prisoner in Rome

> From morning till evening he explained and declared to them the kingdom of God and tried to convince them about Jesus from the Law of Moses and from the Prophets (Acts 28:23).

In this way Christians can find much instruction and great encouragement from the Law if they read it with Christ in mind.

(2) It has a place in conversion

It is often said that the Law's place in the conversion of a sinner to Christ is to convict him of sin. For example, John Flavel wrote:

> … I am assured, till God show you the face of sin in the glass of the law, make the scorpions and fiery serpents that lurk in the law and in your own consciences, to come hissing about you and smiting you with their deadly stings, till you have had some sick nights and sorrowful days, you will never go up and down seeking an interest in the blood of his sacrifice with tears.[30]

---

[30] Flavel, John. *The Works of John Flavel, Vol. 1* (Edinburgh, Banner of Truth, 1968) 152

Also, Calvin wrote:

> … while it shows God's righteousness, that is, the righteousness alone acceptable to God, it warns, informs, convicts, and lastly condemns every man of his own unrighteousness.[31]

This is true only in a limited sense. It convicts of *sins* rather than *sin* itself, which is separation from God. The Law convicts us of breaking it in certain particulars so that we cry out to God, "I have broken your Law, forgive me and help me to stop doing it." So it does not of itself make a sinner realise that he has a fallen nature which is separated from God, irrespective of whether he keeps or breaks the law. It is only conviction of being in a state of separation from God that leads him to seek Christ as a Mediator. The rich young ruler preached the Law to himself, but was not truly convicted until Jesus spoke of following him (Matt. 19:16–22). Later Jesus defined conviction of sin by the Holy Spirit in terms of not believing in him (John 16:8). Paul had an experience of conviction of sin through the Law: In Romans 7:8–24 he wrote of the way it revealed the corruption of his heart and destroyed his self-righteousness. However, he did not preach this in such places as Cyprus, Antioch and Lystra.

Therefore, it is probably true to say that the Law can convict, but it is not sufficient. "God's law does nothing for me but to awaken my bad conscience," (Luther, quoted in Barth on Romans, page 185) James Buchanan wrote

> It is not the bare law as it stands declared in the Ten Commandments that is the sole instrument of conviction; but the moral principle of that law, whether it is displayed in the retributions of a righteous Providence, or illustrated by the afflictions of human life, or exemplified in the conduct of

---

[31] *Institutes* II.vii.6.

believers and the perfect pattern of Christ, or as unfolded in the parables, or as embodied in the Gospel, and shining forth in the Cross. The law is a schoolmaster what [sic] brings the sinner to Christ; but Christ is a teacher that brings the sinner to know the law as he never knew it before.

The law points the eye of a convinced sinner to the cross; but the cross throws in upon his conscience a flood of light which sheds a reflex lustre on the law. **Hence we believe that the Gospel of Christ, especially the doctrine of the Cross of Christ, is the most powerful instrument for impressing the conscience of a sinner, and for turning his convictions into genuine contrition of heart.**[32]

So the Law has a place in the conversion of a sinner by:

- drawing attention to sin (Rom. 3:20, 7:7, 13);
- provoking sin, and thus proving our moral inability (Rom. 7:8–11);
- declaring that sinners are accountable to God (Rom. 2:2–3), and
- creating a sense of the need of a Saviour (Rom. 7:24).

(3) It is a pattern for life

The view of many Reformed confessions is that, while the Law is no longer a "covenant of works" for believers, "it is of great use to them…as a rule of life."[33] This is called the *usus normativus*. Calvin wrote:

The third principal use which pertains more closely to the proper purpose of the Law, finds its place among believers in whose hearts the Spirit of God already lives and reigns. For even though they have the law written and engraved upon their hearts by the finger of God (Jer. 31:33, Heb. 10:16), that is,

---

[32] James Buchanan, *The Office and Work of the Holy Spirit* (Edinburgh: John Johnstone, 1844) 121.

[33] *Westminster Confession of Faith*, XIX, vi.

have been so moved and quickened through the directing of the Spirit that they long to obey God, they still profit by the law in two ways.

[1] Here is the least instrument for them to learn more thoroughly each day the nature of the Lord's will to which they aspire, and confirm them in their understanding of it....

[2] Again, because we need not only teaching but also exhortation, the servant of God will avail himself of this benefit of the law: by frequent meditation on it.[34]

This view, however, has to be heavily qualified to avoid imposing on believers Laws which are over-restrictive or have no clear relevance to the Christian life, such as the dietary Laws and others that involved fine distinctions. The usual way of obviating this difficulty is to make the threefold division referred to earlier between moral, ceremonial and civil laws and to claim that, whereas the last two are abolished, the former remain in force. The reasons for rejecting this division have already been given and they cast doubt on the view of the Law as a rule of life for believers.

At the same time we have to avoid the danger of casting it off altogether as totally irrelevant under the new covenant. This was done from time to time in the history of the church by various advocates of antinomianism.[35] A better view is to call it a *pattern* rather than a *rule* in the sense that our obligations under the new covenant are *in the same areas* as those under the old covenant. Ephesians 6:1–3 is often quoted as proving that Christian believers are just as obligated to the Ten Commandments as were those under the old covenant. Paul here is addressing the children of the churches he is writing to and telling them to "obey your parents," in connection with which he quotes the fifth

---

[34] *Institutes*, II.vii.12.

[35] For further details, see page 135.

commandment. However, the reason he gives for this instruction is "this is right," different from that in the fifth commandment, which is couched in old covenant language concerning the land. He is giving as his authority for his call an eternal moral principle –right–which the fifth commandment recognised. The commandment is not the ultimate authority. What Ephesians 6:1–3 shows is that New Testament ethics covers areas similar to those of Old Testament ethics.

Many laws are about **personal behaviour**: what God requires, especially in our relationships with other people. The last six commandments are the basic ones and applied in detail in subsequent chapters of the Pentateuch. The New Testament also has a great deal about how a believer under the new covenant is to behave. Christ himself set out the basics of this in his Sermon on the Mount and subsequent ethical teaching. The apostles took it even further in their letters. Paul's frequent method was to teach the great doctrines of the Gospel in the early part of his letters, then apply them to behaviour in the second part. The letter to the Romans is written on this pattern, for there is a clear distinction between chapters 1–11 and 12–16. Likewise, the letter to the Ephesians divides neatly into chapters 1–3 and 4–6.

Other laws are about **the worship of God**. The first four commandments come into this category and are followed up by elaborate detail about how God is to be approached. This is probably the largest section of the Law code and the greater part of it is addressed to priests and Levites appointed for this purpose. Of particular importance is how sin is dealt with so that God can be approached acceptably. Under the new covenant this special class of priests is abolished and replaced by the one priest, Christ. Each Christian is a priest in the sense that he has access to God without human interposition, and so the promise that Israel was to be "a kingdom of priests" (Ex. 19:6) comes to fulfilment.

This new principle sweeps away the details of how the worship of God is conducted. But this does not mean the New Testament has nothing to say on this subject. It does, but it concerns attitudes and feelings rather than actions. God is to be **praised** (Matt. 5:16, Rom. 9:5, 1 Cor. 14:16, Eph. 1:6, 12, 14, Heb. 13:15, James 5:13, 1 Pet. 4:11), but there are no set forms of words or books of praise such as the Psalms. This does not mean the Psalms are no longer for use in Christian praise; they are, along with other compositions which appeared in early times, as Paul wrote:

> *Speak to one another in psalms, hymns and spiritual songs. Sing and make music in your heart to the Lord, always giving thanks to God the Father for everything, in the name of our Lord Jesus Christ* (Eph. 5:19–20).

There are even traces of such compositions in the New Testament: 1 Corinthians 13 and Philippians 2:6–11 may have been songs circulating in the churches.

Mainly, however, the New Testament is concerned with the *spirit* of praise. In John 4 Jesus answered the Samaritan woman's enquiry about the appropriate place in which to worship by referring to the nature of God as Spirit (John 4:24). The only way to worship him therefore is "in spirit" (cf. 1 Cor. 14:15). So instead of detailed instructions about forms and words we have exhortations to greater fervency in worship. The above quotation from Ephesians 5 exhorts us to "make music *in your heart* to the Lord," and Colossians 3:16 speaks of singing "with gratitude *in your hearts.*" Mary set the tone with her response to the annunciation:

> *My soul glories in the Lord and my spirit rejoices in God my Saviour* (Luke 1:46–47).

This does not mean the Psalms are lacking in this inward aspect of worship, for Mary's words echo Psalm 103:

> *Praise the Lord, O my soul; all my inmost being, praise his holy name.*

As well as praised, God is also to be **prayed to.** The references to prayer in the New Testament are too numerous to list, and every Christian knows at least a few of these. Apart from the Lord's Prayer, we do not have prayers spelt out to us; there is no fixed liturgy. Again, the concern is with the spirit, which, as with praise, is based on the nature of God. Because he is our Father in heaven we approach him in a spirit of dependence and trust, as Jesus said in Luke 11:11–13:

> *Which of you fathers, if your son asks for a fish, will give him a snake instead? Or if he asks for an egg, will give him a scorpion? If you then, though you are evil, know how to give good gifts to your children, how much more will your Father in heaven give the Holy Spirit to those who ask him?*

The New Testament also points out a whole host of matters which we can and should pray for: from our daily bread to our fierce encounter with the powers of darkness (Eph. 6:18).

The Mosaic law also contains instructions about how Israel was to **operate as a nation**, which apply both to rulers and ruled. Crime and punishment are strong themes and occur in other books, such as Proverbs. The New Testament does likewise, although it does not directly address rulers, since the church is not a state in the way Israel was. It is possible to deduce the functions of rulers, but it is addressed more to the ruled than to the rulers. It gives specific instructions to the Christians about how they are to behave in society, including their responsibility to those who are over them. Paul, along with all other Christians at that time, lived under the Roman Emperor Nero, but unhesitatingly bade Christians to "submit to the governing authorities"

(Rom. 13:1–7). Those to whom he wrote lived at the very heart of where Nero exercised his power with great cruelty and injustice (the city of Rome), yet he even calls him "God's servant to do you good." Peter wrote to Christians in the more remote parts of the Empire, but gave similar instructions: 1 Peter 2:13–17. Christians and churches can flourish under the worst regimes. They can even live the Christian life under a slave system: 1 Peter 2:18–25! Christians are not to take the law into their own hands in changing regimes or reforming society. God will do this in his own way and time. As regards evil governments, the book of Revelation is very clear what God thinks of them and will do to them!

It is also possible to see in the civil or judicial Laws of Moses principles that can guide in the ordering and administering of the affairs of the church of Christ. This applies particularly to its government and various ministries. More will be said about this in the Chapter 10.

So, although the detailed instructions in the New Testament are very different from those in the Old Testament, they cover the same areas of life. They need to be adapted to life in the age of the kingdom. They were adequate for old covenant times but need adaptation in the way the apostles used them. For example, Paul applied the Law about not muzzling the ox to the payment of preachers (1 Cor. 9:9–10). Our Christian life is lived by walking with a Father, not by carrying out a set of rules.

The Law of Sinai is not replaced with antinomianism, a condition in which all law is absent, but with what Paul called "the law of Christ" (Gal. 6:2). Paul's position in relation to the Law of God was that, although he was not under the Law (of Moses), he became *like* one such (the Jew), if necessary, in order to win him. To those not under the

Law (Gentiles) he became *like* them, which he qualifies by saying he was "not free from God's law but under Christ's law" (1 Cor. 9:19–21). This is the Christian position. Some Puritans understood the phrase *under the law of Christ* to mean that it is the same Law as that given at Sinai but we receive it from Christ rather than from Moses. But this would mean we are still under the Law of Moses, including all the detailed restrictions which no Puritan ever wished to impose on us. **Our rule of life is not the Ten Commandments but the whole Bible.**

(C) Its purpose for the world generally

(Much of what was said on pages 40–45 under "The Abiding Value of the Law for Israel" is applicable here).

Although the Law was not issued to the other nations of the world, it was never totally unknown to them. Moses when he recited the Law to Israel told them that if they

> *Observe them carefully...this will show your wisdom and understanding to the nations, who will hear about all these decrees and say, "Surely this is a wise and understanding people."*
>
> *...what other nation is so great as to have such righteous decrees and laws as this body of Laws I am setting before you today?* (Deut. 4:6, 8).

As the centuries went by and Israel became increasingly involved with other nations, so its Law-code became more and more widely known. The Old Testament became translated into other languages and was thus read or heard by many people. Since the coming of Christ this process has accelerated, so that a vast section of the world's population has some idea that there is a God who has revealed his will for man. The majority may embrace some other faith, but the Law still serves his purposes for the world generally.

(a) It teaches what God is like

The law of God comes from his own nature; it is the revelation of his mind and will. God **is** the law, the perfect standard. What God is and does constitutes the law. There is no abstract standard outside of God to which he must conform, no court of appeal by which he can be judged. What he says and does is in and of itself right.

More particularly

- It reveals a God who is *holy, righteous and just.* As seen from the above quotation from Deuteronomy, it was the boast of Israel that it alone had a Law which was wholly righteous because it came from a God who is wholly righteous. What God is in himself is what he requires from creatures which he made in his likeness. So he commands holiness for the simple reason that he himself is holy, that is, absolutely pure, without blemish or defect:

Be holy because I am holy (Lev. 11:44–45, 19:2).

- It reveals a God who, because he is *love*, is *understanding and sympathetic.* There is much in the Law that shows his understanding and sympathy for the needy and vulnerable: widows and orphans (Deut. 10:18), aliens (Deut. 10:19), the poor (Lev. 19:13, Deut. 24:14–15, 19–21), the blind and the afflicted (Lev. 19:14). He understands what it must be like to lose an animal which strays or falls, and requires someone who finds it to restore it to its owner (Deut. 22:1–4). He does not allow a creditor to deprive a labouring man of his tools or his bedclothes (Deut. 24:6, 12–13). He even excuses the newly married from military service (Deut. 24:5)!

- It reveals a God who is *in control.* As Creator and Lord of the earth and all that is in it he has the right to issue commands and require obedience to them. He need give no other justification for this than his own authority. This is seen particularly in Leviticus 19 which, after some of the particular commands, has the repeated refrain "I am the Lord your God." But God is not arbitrarily authoritarian in the way human dictators tend to be. There is always good reason for the laws he gives. Without law the world would fall into chaos. Not only does anarchy not work, it has never been seriously tried.

(b) It teaches what man is like

- It shows that man has a basic *sense of right and wrong, justice and injustice,* to which appeals can be made. Man is basically a moral creature; he has a conscience. He has a sense of what he and others should be. So he tends to judge others, and even himself, as Paul did in Romans 7, when he spoke of not doing the things he wished to do, and doing the things he wished not to do. He felt like a prisoner to this law or principle, condemned and awaiting the punishment of death.

- It shows that man is one who has *fallen from his ideal,* who qualifies for the name sinner, for "by the law is the knowledge of sin" or "by the law we become conscious of sin" (Rom. 3:20).

> *Law is made not for the righteous but for law-breakers and rebels, for the unholy and irreligious, for those who kill their fathers and mothers, for murderers, for adulterers and perverts, for slave-traders and liars and perjurers—and for whatever is contrary to the sound doctrine* (1 Tim. 1:9–10).

This is not to say there is no sense at all in which the Law of Moses is relevant to Christians, but that this is not its main function in this age, which is to convict and restrain non-Christians. Paul's use of the word *righteous* here is similar to that of Christ in Matthew 9:13: "I have not come to call the righteous but sinners." He was answering the Pharisees who were criticising his consorting with tax-collectors and sinners rather than with such as the Pharisees. "The righteous" therefore are the *self-righteous* who claim they are justified by their obedience to the Law. Paul attacks the whole idea of justification by works in Romans and Galatians. The Law was not intended to justify those who think they obey it and claim to be righteous through it. On the contrary, the Law draws attention to those sins mentioned in the above verse (among others). "The primary purpose of the law was to deal with wrong-doing."[36]

Dr Kevan's understanding of this verse is that, like the rest of the Bible, "it teaches that it was the entrance of sin into the world that provided the occasion for the formal proclamation of the law."[37] This means that it was sin in the human race that necessitated the Sinai legislation. This is connected to the original sin of Adam. He sinned against a specific or *positive law*. That law no longer applies, since there is no Garden of Eden or tree of knowledge. But his sin was imputed to his descendants and that created a general lawless attitude to God. Man began to rebel against God's *natural law*, necessitating a written code.

- It shows that man is *accountable for his actions*. He feels within himself that because he fails to attain to this ideal of doing right, and frequently does wrong instead, that he will be held responsible and judged adversely for his actions. This applies equally to those who have the Law and those who are ignorant of it, as Paul says in Romans 2:14–15.

So, far from being a dead letter, or a rather tedious and long section of the Scriptures, the Law is integral to the

---

[36] Kevan, *Keep the Commandments,* 27.

[37] Ibid., 15.

whole life of man, and can greatly enrich our thinking and living, if correctly understood.

CHAPTER 6
THE LAW IN THE TEACHING
OF CHRIST

Jesus came to make things new, not just to patch up the defects in the old: Mark 2:21–22. The new wine he brought needed new bottles to contain it. In this he was up against tradition and prejudice, just as we are. We need to clear our minds of these and see things in a new way—a way to which he introduced us. Some of the things Christ said about the Law may *sound* as if it is still in force but we have to remember that there is a sense in which Jesus, as a Jew, had at least one foot in the old covenant. The same applies to his strict adherence to the law of Moses, as was seen in the discussion of his active obedience.

Earlier, five distinct meanings of *law* used in the Bible were discussed. Two of these apply in considering Jesus' teaching on the law. The key idea in both is FULFILMENT.

A. LAW AS THE OLD TESTAMENT SCRIPTURES

The Jews called the Scriptures *Law, Prophets and Writings,* which could be shortened to *Law and Prophets* or just *Law.* The key passage here is Matthew 5:17–20, where Jesus refers to the Scriptures as "the law or the prophets." These he has "come not to abolish but fulfill." The word *fulfill* is PLEROO, translated by Weymouth as "give them their completion."[38] They were not incorrect but they were incomplete. They were true because they were the Word of God, for in John 10:34–35 Jesus equates the Law, the Word of God, and the

---

[38] R.F. Weymouth, *The New Testament in Modern Speech* (London, James Clarke, 1916).

Scriptures. Since the Old Testament Scriptures are the Word of God they must be true. But they are not the whole truth; they are incomplete and find their completion in Christ.

Jesus used the term *fulfill* again after his resurrection in Luke's version of the Great Commission:

> *Everything must be fulfilled that is written about me in the Law of Moses, the prophets and the Psalms* (Luke 24:44).

Shortly before this he had encountered two disciples on the Emmaus road and spelt out the Scriptures he fulfilled, although the word *fulfilled* is not actually used:

> *Beginning with Moses and all the prophets he explained to them what was said in all the Scriptures concerning himself* (Luke 24:27).

In Matthew 11:11–13 he draws a distinction between "the Law and the Prophets" which lasted "until John the Baptist," and the age of "the kingdom of heaven," which began with him.

This distinction is also found in Matthew 5:17–20, where, having spoken of "the Law and the Prophets" in Matthew 5:17–18, Jesus goes on to speak about "the kingdom of heaven" in Matthew 5:19–20. The kingdom of heaven is the age which began with his coming. When he first set out preaching, following the withdrawal of John the Baptist from the scene, his message was:

> *The time has come, the kingdom of God is near; repent and believe the gospel* (Mark 1:14).

The demands of the kingdom are not merely as stringent as those of the Old Testament, as he says in Matthew 5:19, but even surpass them, for those who are in his kingdom have a righteousness which "surpasses that of the Pharisees and teachers of the law" (Matt. 5:20). In Matthew 5:18 he used the word *accomplished*, for it was not just the teaching of the Law that was incomplete but its carrying out. Reference has already been made to the active and passive obedience of Christ: he obeyed the Scriptures perfectly by keeping the Laws (active obedience) and by suffering the punishments (passive obedience). In these ways he accomplished everything in the Scriptures.

This can be further borne out by looking at different themes in the Old Testament.

(1) Israel's History

The history of Israel in the Old Testament is a story with a clear beginning—the call of Abraham—but no clear ending. Their arrival in the Promised Land was not the end, neither was the return to it after the exile in Babylon. From this time they lived under a succession of empires. They remained distinct racially and politically, but enjoyed only limited freedom. This could hardly be the kingdom they had been promised in passages such as Isaiah 2:2–4!

The last historical event recorded of Israel in the Scriptures is the programme of reforms carried out by Nehemiah on his second visit to Jerusalem some time after "the third year of Artaxerxes" (Neh. 13:6), that is, 433 BC. The condition of the people at that time in no way resembled the visions of Isaiah; for example, Nehemiah found the people admitting Ammonites to the congregation, the high priest Eliashib even providing one of their leading men— Tobiah, whose family had intermarried with that of Eliashib—with rooms in the temple! The Levites seem to have vacated the temple and gone home to work their farms, which is probably why they were not being paid. Trading was being conducted on the Sabbath day. Following the example of their high priest, the people of Judah were intermarrying with the neighbouring nations. What an end to a great story!

Isaiah's visions clearly still awaited fulfilment, and the people were still, as they had always been, looking forward to this fulfilment when Christ came. The last prophet, Malachi, who may well have been contemporary with Nehemiah, ended his book by speaking of a *day* when the true people of God, those who "revere his name," will be clearly evident and distinct from all the rest, and "for them the sun of righteousness will rise with healing in his wings" (Mal. 4:2). This event will be accompanied by a terrible judgment on every evildoer. This may refer to AD 70, God's final judgment on the Jewish nation, when many Jews were killed and many others scattered among the nations; for there was no longer any purpose for Israel. They had been raised up to keep alive the knowledge of God and his truth, especially to safeguard the promise of a Redeemer first uttered by the mouth of God himself at the fall (Gen. 3:15), and subsequently revealed to Moses who recorded it in the Scriptures.

Nor was it due to their efforts that the Scriptures were still in existence when Christ came. Time and again the vast bulk of the people, including the kings and other leaders, lost interest in God and his Word, replacing him with idols and his Word with the teachings of false prophets and the incantations of occultists. The Scriptures disappeared altogether for two long periods, only to be recovered when God raised up godly kings—Hezekiah and Josiah. It was due to God's grace and providence that the Scriptures were there at all when the time of their fulfilment came! Stephen, the first martyr, put it very bluntly when, after outlining the history of Israel, he said to the Jewish leaders

> *You stiff-necked people, with uncircumcised hearts and ears! You are just like your fathers: you always resist the Holy Spirit! Was there ever a prophet your fathers did not persecute? They even killed those who prophesied the coming of the Righteous One. And now you have betrayed and murdered him—you who have received the law*

that was put into effect through angels but have not obeyed it (Acts 7:51–53).

So the nation of Israel did not complete God's purpose.

2) Israel's characters

Israel had some great men down the ages, but all were flawed. They never attained their goals or received what was promised them:

All these people were still living by faith when they died. They did not receive the things promised; they only saw them and welcomed them from a distance. And they admitted they were only aliens and strangers on earth (Heb. 11:13).

Abraham was promised an inheritance which he never received. He was promised a city, but "lived in a tent" (Heb. 11:9). He was promised descendants "as numerous as the stars in the sky" (Heb. 11:12), but had only 2 sons, of which he nearly lost the more important one. Even this incident with Isaac had an incompleteness about it. Isaac was not "raised from the dead" because he never quite died! Jesus went beyond Isaac—he both died and rose. It was this that led to the promise of numerous descendants and a heavenly city and country, to which such as Abraham were continually looking forward:

... he was looking forward to the city with foundations, whose architect and builder is God...

People who say such things show they are looking for a country of their own. If they had been thinking of the country they had left, they would have had opportunity to return. Instead they were looking for a better country - a heavenly one (Heb. 11:10, 14–16).

Israel never attained a population comparable to "the stars in the sky" or "the sand by the sea shore." In fact they tended to dwindle as time went by, as the genealogies show. Less than 50,000 returned from captivity in Babylon. But the heavenly city and country established by Jesus comprises "a great multitude which no one can count" (Rev. 7:9), a statement which immediately follows one in which the tribes of Israel are said to number 144,000. It is true this is a symbolic number, but it is countable and limited. The writer to the Hebrews explains this. It was not that the faith of these men was defective; in fact he "commends their faith" (Heb. 11:2). The reason was that

> *God had planned something better for us, so that only together with us would they be made perfect* (Heb. 11:40).

(3) Israel's rituals

Jesus never denounced the ceremonies of the law. He respected them: he sent the healed leper off to the priests to fulfill their requirements (Mark 1:44). But he did claim to surpass and fulfill them. When he referred to the ministry of the priests in the temple he said

> *One greater than the Temple is here* (Matt. 12:6).

Later on, he prophesied that the temple—which he was greater than—would be razed to the ground (Matt. 24). In John 2:19–21 he spoke of his body as the Temple. Whereas the Jews would never rebuild the temple which is to be destroyed in AD 70, as he himself prophesied in Matthew 24, his Temple would be raised in three days. The rituals of the Law never achieved perfect forgiveness and salvation. His death and resurrection would, for they were a finished or accomplished work. The rituals of the Law were shadows (Heb. 10:1) of which he and his work were the substance. Matthew 15:1–20 shows this in relation to ritual washing.

(4) Israel's Prophets

Many of the predictions of the prophets were fulfilled either in their own time or subsequently during the centuries before Christ. But there is much more to them that this.

Some were never fulfilled during the Old Testament period. For example, there is much discussion as to what Isaiah 53 is referring to, and indeed the *suffering servant* passages generally. If there was a fulfilment prior to Christ, it is difficult to find it.

Some prophecies have a double fulfilment: a partial one in the times prior to Christ, but a fuller one in him, when they received their ultimate fulfilment. For example, Isaiah prophesies (Isa. 7:14) the birth of a child whose name was to be *Emmanuel* (God with us). This was intended to give assurance to Judah that the Israel-Syria coalition will not overcome them because God was on their side. This happened, and so the prophecy received its immediate fulfilment. But Matthew 1:21 also quoted this when Joseph was told of the forthcoming birth of a son to Mary though she was still a virgin. He was told to call him *Jesus*, but Matthew quotes Isaiah 7:14 to declare that this Jesus will be Emmanuel, God with us, not to save the Jews from foreign enemies but all mankind from their sins. This was the ultimate fulfilment of Isaiah's prophecy.

Other such prophecies quoted by Matthew and fulfilled by Jesus are in: Matthew 2:15, 18, 23, 4:15–16, 8:17 and 21:4–5. Jesus himself also quoted prophecies fulfilled by him in: Matthew 21:42, 22:41–45, 26:54, and Luke 4:16–21. Thus, wherever we look in the Old Testament—to narratives, to Laws and ceremonies, to characters or to prophecies, we see how they are completed or fulfilled in Christ. (For more about the meaning of *fulfill* see the Appendix on Matthew 5:17-20).

B. THE LAW AS COMMANDMENTS

The term *law* is also used in the more limited sense of the commandments given by God to Moses on Sinai. Jesus referred to this in the same passage as that in which he refers to the Law as the Scriptures: Matthew 5:17–20. (This passage is explained in detail in the Appendix.) Having said in Matthew 5:17–18 that he has come to fulfill "the Law and the Prophets" (the Scriptures) both in general and in detail, he goes on to speak of "the commandments" (Matt. 5:19).

What are these commandments? The Puritans and many Reformed theologians since then take the view that Jesus' words in Matthew 5 prefixed by "I tell you" are implicit in the Decalogue. But it seems more likely that they are the commandments of the kingdom, Jesus' own commandments. Moses predicted the coming of a prophet like himself (Deut. 18:15–20). He will speak the words that God gives him, as Moses did. He will have the authority of Moses so that anyone who refuses to hear him will be called to account. Christ was a greater Law-giver than Moses whom he replaces. This is demonstrated in Matthew 5:17-48 when he uses the words *But I tell you*, and in the exhortations in Matthew 6–7, which begin with words in the imperative mood, words of command beginning "Be careful…" (Matt. 6:1). These occur frequently throughout the Gospels, along with the expression "I tell you the truth," as in John 3:3. Then there are those which actually use the word *command* (verb) or *commandments* (noun) in John 14–17 (as mentioned in the Appendix on Matthew 5:17-20). This is why he speaks of "the kingdom of heaven" in each of the three verses in Matthew 5:19–21. Before Christ God's reign or kingdom was confined to one nation. This is not to say his sovereign rule did not extend to other nations of the world, for as God of creation and providence he rules not only over this planet but all the bodies in the universe.

What this means is that God has only **revealed** his sovereign will to one nation, spelling out what he promised and what he required. Only this one nation acknowledged his sovereign rule and called him their *King*, even though they frequently backslid and even apostatised from him. But since the coming of Christ, his will has been revealed to people of all nations through the gospel. These commandments he is about to give are for all who will come under God's sway through Christ. It is those who do and teach these who are in the kingdom of heaven. It is their obedience to them that determines their position in the kingdom. Greatness is no longer a matter of rank, title, wealth and office, as it was at this time in all the nations and to some extent among the Jews, but of knowledge of and obedience to the commandments of Jesus.

Moreover, these commandments now form the definition of *righteousness*: Matthew 5:20. At the time righteousness was defined in terms of observing the Laws of Moses, as augmented by the teachings of the rabbis in the Mishnah, and of which the Pharisees and teachers of the Law were the foremost exponents. Jesus said the righteousness of the members of his kingdom must surpass that. What that meant became clear when he spelt out what his commandments were. They were based on the commandments of Sinai but went much deeper. The Ten Commandments as they stand, apart from the tenth, are purely external and relate to conduct. The commandments of Jesus cover inward attitudes, feelings and motives. For example, not only is the act of murder wrong, but so is hatred, whether or not it ever leads to a violent act. Not only is the act of adultery wrong, but so are sexual fantasies. Not only is oath-breaking wrong, but so is all idle swearing. This is the righteousness which those in the kingdom are to seek: Matthew 6:33.

This new law of Christ constituted a new covenant. As we have already seen, the Law of Sinai spelt out the terms of the covenant between God and Israel. God had created this nation to safeguard his promise of redemption. They were in a special relationship with God at a time when he was virtually unknown to other nations. Abraham himself, when God called him, "worshipped other gods" (Josh. 24:2). God revealed himself to Abraham and made great promises to him: a nation will come from him which would eventually be the means of bringing his blessing to the whole earth (Gen. 12:1–3). God entered into a covenant with Abraham, at the heart of which was the promise of a son. On his part Abraham must believe the promise and circumcise his offspring as a token of his faith.

Eventually the promise was fulfilled and the descendants of Abraham gradually increased until they became a nation, a special one, "a holy nation" (Ex. 19:5). But it was not until they were released from captivity in Egypt and became a free and independent people that God established his covenant with them at Sinai. On his part God promised to keep them as his own people by giving them their own land. On their part, they promised to keep the Laws he revealed there (Ex. 19:8). The Mosaic covenant was to a considerable extent about the tenure of land. Obedience will secure it and make it fruitful; disobedience will bring curses on it and ultimately its loss. This is why, when the covenant came to an end so did Israel's tenure of the land. This covenant would mark them out as different from other people and thus be a witness to the true and holy God. After the Law had been declared and inscribed on stone tablets, the covenant was confirmed with the shedding and sprinkling of bull's blood (Ex. 24). Since that generation died out during the forty years in the desert, the covenant had to be renewed with the generation who would actually enter the land. This was done in an even more elaborate form, as recorded in Deuteronomy 26:16–30:20, in fact it could be extended to the remainder of Deuteronomy.

Once made, this covenant was to last until the promised Messiah came. As John wrote in his preface

> The law was given by Moses, but grace and truth came by Jesus Christ (John 1:17).

Moses' ministry was of the Law, but it pointed to Christ, as Jesus said: "Moses wrote about me" (John 5:46)—not in plain language but in types and shadows. When the Messiah came the ministry of Moses would give way to that of Christ, which would be a ministry of grace and truth. Paul put it another way in Romans 10:4:

> Christ is the end of the law so that there may be righteousness for everyone who believes.

The word *end* is used in two senses here. **First**, it means *realisation* or *fulfilment*. Christ carried out all its demands and did so for our righteousness—his active obedience is imputed to us; we become righteous by faith in him, which we could not do by obeying the Law. In Romans 3:31 Paul concludes his discussion on justification through faith rather than Law by saying faith "establishes the law." This carries the same meaning as *end* in Romans 10:4 and *fulfill* in Matthew 5:17. Faith in Christ was what the Law was pointing to. **Second,** it means *termination*, because he brought to an end the Law's demands on us through his passive obedience. This refers to the Sinai law not the eternal moral law, which remains in force. E.F. Kevan suggests "the law considered dispensationally receives its *terminus* in the fulfilment of its spiritual purpose in directing the sinner to his refuge in Christ."[39]

The Law was not an end in itself, but pointed and led to the promised Messiah. This was to change the way of righteousness from Law-keeping to believing. "By the coming of faith the law was abolished."[40] The Law period

---

[39] Kevan, *Keep His Commandments*, 26.

terminated with John (Matt. 11:13). Law was king up to that time, after which Christ was king (Luke 16:16). Just as the way of righteousness through the Law was put in the form of a covenant, so was the way of righteousness through faith in Christ. As the old covenant was established through blood, so was the new covenant, as Jesus himself said when he transformed the Passover, an old covenant ceremony, into the Lord's Supper, a new covenant ceremony:

> *This cup is the new covenant in my blood which is poured out for you* (Luke 22:20).

This new covenant was itself prophesied in connection with the coming Messianic kingdom in Jeremiah 31:31–34. While Jeremiah does not refer to Christ or to blood, he does stress the inwardness of this covenant as compared with the externality of the old.

Jesus spelt out that this covenant was based on his death on the cross. It was to be that act which performed all that was needed, hinted at, and promised in the old covenant. So, whereas the old covenant looked forward to a time when it will be fulfilled or completed, the new covenant looks back to a work which has been completed. This was why Jesus used the word *remember*, a backward-looking word. All the unresolved problems and incomplete acts of forgiveness had been brought to an end. The old covenant gives way to the new:

> *By calling this covenant "new" he* [Jeremiah, or God through Jeremiah] *has made the first one obsolete, and what is obsolete and aging will soon disappear* (Heb. 8:13).

A new covenant, based on a new way of acceptance with God through a new priesthood, also necessitates a new law, for

---

[40] Calvin, *Institutes*, III.ii.6.

For when there is a change of priesthood, there must also be a change of law (Heb. 7:12).

Hebrews 8:7–8 explains why the change was needed.

For if there had been nothing wrong with that first covenant, no place would have been sought for another. But God found fault with the people and said:

"The time is coming, declares the Lord,
when I will make a new covenant

with the house of Israel

and with the house of Judah."

The Westminster Confession (XIX.iv) states that the "judicial laws" given to Israel, like the ceremonial ones have expired or been abrogated. However, in its Scripture proofs it juxtaposes Matthew 5:17 with Matthew 5:38–39. This shows that it understands *fulfill* in Matthew 5:17 as meaning *show the ultimate purpose of* and must therefore apply to the Law **as a whole**. The statement is qualified by the use of the term *general equity*. The judicial Laws of Sinai are thus seen as still applicable in situations where the demands of justice require them.

This brings us back to Matthew 5:17–20. Jesus has fulfilled, accomplished or completed all that the Law was trying to achieve (Matt. 5:17–18). On this basis he has instituted the kingdom of heaven, and thus has enlarged and renewed the old kingdom of Israel (Matt. 5:19). Those who come into this kingdom and obey its commandments have a righteousness which exceeds the best that could be achieved under the old covenant (Matt. 5:20).

Jesus then proceeded to give examples of the commandments of the kingdom of heaven (Matt. 5:21–42), and then summed it all up in the word *love* (Matt. 5:43–48). This love is the way to be "perfect as your heavenly Father is perfect." This is not sinless or faultless perfection but fullness, maturity, completion. We are not expected to be "**as** perfect as our heavenly Father," but perfect **in the way** our heavenly Father is perfect, that is, in the spirit of love. Christ's new covenant and new law are the completion or fulfilment of what came before. So those with whom it is made reach the fullest state of righteousness and likeness to God which it is possible for earthly and fleshly man to attain—that is, the state of love. When God made man in his image, our relationship with him was one of trust and love. That love died at the fall. It is restored by Christ through the love which took him to the cross. Later he was to spell this out even more plainly, for shortly before he suffered he declared his "new commandment" (John 13:34–35). This commandment is the sum and essence of the whole Law:

> *...an expert in the law tested him with this question: "Teacher, which is the greatest commandment in the Law?" Jesus replied, "Love the Lord your God with all your heart and with all your soul and with all your mind. This is the first and greatest commandment. And the second is like it: Love your neighbour as yourself. All the Law and the Prophets hang on these two commandments"* (Matt. 22:35–40).

This love is the fruit of the Holy Spirit (Gal. 5:22) who is "poured into the hearts" of those who are "justified by faith" (Rom. 5:5) and thus in Christ's new covenant.

Matthew 6–7 enlarges on the commandments of the kingdom with duties such as almsgiving, prayer and fasting: Matthew 6:1–18. Personal trust in God as Father also characterises the lives of citizens of Christ's kingdom: Matthew 6:25–34. There is also the humility that refrains from judging others but judges itself: Matthew 7:1–5.This does not make naiveté or gullibility a virtue, for he also instructs members of his kingdom to "watch out for false prophets" (Matt. 7:6, 15–23). He ends by coming back to his original idea of cultivating a righteousness which exceeds that of the Law by telling us to build our whole life on his words: Matthew 7:24–27.

CHAPTER 7
LAW AND GOSPEL

Mr. [Patrick] Hamelton well knew that half of our religious mistakes arise from not clearly ascertaining the difference between the law and the gospel, and from not exactly distinguishing the true nature of each. This he does with great judgment and accuracy in the following remarks.

The law saith, Pay thy debt (the debt of perfect obedience to God). The gospel saith, Christ hath paid it.

The law saith, thou art a sinner; despair and thou shalt be damned. The gospel says, thy sins be forgiven thee, be of comfort and thou shalt be saved.

The law saith, Make amends for thy sins. The gospel saith, Christ hath made it for thee.

The law saith, the Father of Heaven is angry with thee. The gospel saith, Christ hath pacified him with his blood.

The law saith, where is thy righteousness, goodness and satisfaction? The gospel saith, Christ is thy righteousness, goodness and satisfaction.

The law saith, thou art bound [over] to me, to the Devil and to Hell. The gospel saith, Christ hath delivered thee from them all.[41]

I am still using the term *Law* in the sense of the code of rules given by God to Israel through Moses on Mount Sinai. The term *Gospel* (literally *good tidings* or *good news*) refers to the message accompanying the arrival of the promised Messiah, first announced by an angel to shepherds in Luke 2:10–11:

---

[41] William Tyndale, *Works* (London, publisher unknown, 1861)

*Do not be afraid. I bring you good news of great joy that will be
for all the people. Today in the town of David a Saviour has been born
to you; he is Christ the Lord.*

The term for *good news* is actually a verb, and would read
literally "I evangelise you a great joy." The meaning of these
words which announced his arrival was expounded by
Christ during the course of his earthly ministry, and more
fully by his apostles after he had carried out the work
necessary to his office of Saviour.

This means that the Sinai code of Laws was temporary,
lasting only from Sinai until the coming of the promised
kingdom of Christ, first preached by John the Baptist:

*The law and the prophets were proclaimed until John. Since that
time the good news (gospel) of the kingdom is being preached* (Luke
16:16).

Again the word used for *good news* is a verb: the
"kingdom is being evangelised." The *good news* of the
kingdom contrasts with the stringency of the Law code:

*It is easier for heaven and earth to disappear than for the least
stroke of a pen to drop out of the law* (Luke 16:17).

The Law was not abrogated but fulfilled, as he said in
Luke 24:44:

*This is what I told you when I was still with you. Everything
must be fulfilled which was written about me in the Law of Moses,
the Prophets and the Psalms.*

Luke 16:18 then shows how Jesus' teaching transcended
the Law in the matter of divorce. One school of rabbis was
virtually teaching what we would call no-fault divorce. But
Jesus sought to restore God's original intention of
monogamous life-long marriage:

*"Haven't you read," he replied, "that at the beginning the Creator
'made them male and female,' and said, 'For this reason a man will
leave his father and mother and be united to his wife, and the two will*

become one flesh'? So they are no longer two, but one. Therefore what God has joined together, let man not separate" (Matt. 19:4–6).

Jesus' transcending of the Law is put in another way by John the apostle in the prologue of his gospel:

> *The law was given through Moses, but grace and truth came through Jesus Christ* (John 1:17).

When Christ came the emphasis in God's dealings changed from law to grace. There *is* grace in law; since it was given by God and all his gifts are in grace. The Law shows us how to live a life of which God approves, which attracts his blessing, which shows us how to keep out of trouble and many other things, as described in Chapter 3. But the grace in the Law was not full grace. Full grace "came," that is, it is not a written code but a living person, none other than Christ, the promised Redeemer, the divine and human One.

There are a number of ways in which the contrast between Law and Gospel can be brought out.

A. THE LAW WAS FOR THE KINGDOM OF ISRAEL, THE GOSPEL FOR THE KINGDOM OF GOD.

The Law governed the way God dealt with Israel, whereas the gospel is his good news for all nations. It has already been described how Sinai Law constituted the covenant between God and the nation he created through Abraham, Isaac and Jacob. It stipulated what God expected from the people in terms of personal behaviour and corporate worship, and it made many promises of blessings from God. But God had other and greater plans, not just for Israel but for the whole human race, as he said to Abraham when he first called him:

> *All peoples of the earth will be blessed through you* (Gen. 12:3).

Israel was created to receive these promises and preserve them until the time came for them to be fulfilled. Paul puts it thus:

They have been entrusted with the very words of God (Rom. 3:2).

This he developed in Romans 9:4–5:

Theirs is the adoption as sons; theirs the divine glory, the covenants, the receiving of the law, the temple worship and the promises. Theirs are the patriarchs, and from them is the human ancestry of Christ, who is God over all, forever praised! Amen.

"The promises" (Rom. 9:5) refer to the promises of a Redeemer; promises first made in Eden after the fall (Gen. 3:15) and repeated in many different ways down the following centuries. Indeed there is a sense in which the promises were enshrined in the very life of the nation, with its experience of bondage in Egypt and its miraculous release.

The promise was later called *a new covenant* (Jer. 31:31–34). This covenant contrasts with the Sinai covenant chiefly in that it is internal, not written on stone tables but on the heart. It promised a forgiveness of sins that far exceeded what Israel ever knew. In fact, the very method of forgiveness under the law was also a reminder of sin:

These sacrifices are an annual reminder of sins, because it is impossible for the blood of bulls and goats to take away sins (Heb. 10:3–4).

Under the new covenant, sins are "remembered no more" (Jer. 31:34, Heb. 8:13). This is why the New Testament says that Christ came to do what the Law was powerless to do: Romans 8:1–4, 10:4, Hebrews 10:1–3.

The terms of the new covenant are therefore primarily inward, though they have outward manifestations. They all relate to the One who came to bring the redemption that was typified in the exodus from Egypt, and to fulfill the promises of forgiveness in Jeremiah 31:34. These terms are faith in Christ, love for Christ and obedience to Christ. It is in these terms that people everywhere are called to Christ and offered pardon. Paul said he had "received grace and apostleship to bring about the obedience of faith among all nations" (Rom. 1:5 ESV).

The expression "obedience of faith" brings out the contrast between Law and Gospel. The Law required the performance of works, the Gospel calls for faith.

> The apostle therefore bears witness to the Gospel: that it is the word of faith. He distinguishes the Gospel both from the precepts of the Law and the promises, since there is nothing that can establish faith except the generous embassy by which God reconciles the world to himself.[42]

That no more than this was required was made clear at the Council of Jerusalem in Acts 15. Some Jewish Christians were demanding that Gentile believers should be circumcised and keep the whole Law of Moses. But the apostles and elders decreed that the only requirements should be abstinence from idolatry, murder and immorality (Acts 15:28–29). The reference to the "meat of strangled animals" was a concession to the Jews who still took the eating of flesh with the blood literally, but this gradually dropped out and is not mentioned in later references to the Jerusalem Council's rulings. Also, the Council did not impose the Laws of the Decalogue on Gentiles. An example of this contrast is seen in the changed policy on mixed marriage. Jews had been required to divorce their non-Jewish wives (Ezra 10), but Christians were advised to try to keep their marriage with non-Christians together (1 Cor. 7:12–13).

---

[42] Calvin, *Institutes*: III.ii.29.

Although the Gospel was to surpass the Law, the period in which the people of God were under the Law was by no means unimportant; in fact it was an essential preparation for the gospel in several ways.

1. *The law created the nation from which the Messiah Saviour and King was to come.* It was the Law more than anything else which made Israel distinct from the other nations (Deut. 4:5–8). It was from a specially favoured nation, indeed a nation miraculously created by God himself that the new King and his kingdom would arise. The Law acted as a kind of governor or guardian of the nation until it reached maturity in the coming of Christ: Galatians 3:23–24, 4:3. The word translated *schoolmaster* in the KJV and paraphrased in the NIV as *put in charge* is *paidagōgos.* This person in the Roman Empire at that time was a kind of permanent *childminder* who took the young children off the parents' hands until they were older. The old covenant with Israel, therefore, was seen as the minority or childhood period of the people of God. Just as rules are essential to the young, so the Law was essential to Israel before the coming of the kingdom of Christ.

2. *The law prepared the way for the gospel by its teaching on sin.* People of other nations had only their consciences and were wildly inaccurate in their ideas of sin; many things forbidden by God's Laws were permissible to them, and many things that were taboo to them were permitted by God. Only Israel through its Law had a correct definition of sin.

3. *The law also prepared the way for the gospel in that it enshrined the person of Christ.* Being a perfect code, one who kept it would be a perfect man. But no one did

keep it perfectly until Christ himself came, who at his baptism said

It is proper for us to fulfill all righteousness (Matt. 3:15).

He claimed always to do what pleased the Father (John 8:20). Paul said he was "born under the law" (Gal. 4:4) and the Gospels show how from the very beginning everything he did or was done to him was "required by the law of the Lord" (Luke 2:39). One of his closest colleagues, Peter, said of him

He committed no sin and no deceit was found in his mouth (1 Pet. 2:22).

This itself was a quotation from Isaiah 53:9, showing how Law and prophets concur in their description of Christ.

4. *The law depicted the way in which Christ was to achieve our redemption.* Knowing that none would perfectly keep his Law, God provided a way of pardon for sins against it: the ceremony of offering an animal in the place of the sinner. This is the basis for the New Testament's teaching on atonement by a substitutionary sacrifice. John the Baptist first announced this when he declared

Look, the Lamb of God who takes away the sin of the world! (John 1:29).

The apostles explained this in greater detail, for example:

God presented him as a sacrifice of atonement, through faith in his blood (Rom. 3:25).

The letter to the Hebrews is even more expansive, especially in Chapter 10.

All this shows us how the gospel is the only way appropriate to the universal kingdom that Christ set up. God created a small nation through which to reveal what he purposed to do. In this the Law played an important part. But it did not accomplish redemption, even for that one nation, let alone for the nations of the world. That work had to be done by God himself through his Son coming personally among us. But the period of Law was significant in preparing the way for this, bringing out the principles on which it would be based.

Unhappily, instead of seeing their responsibility to witness to the God who had revealed himself and his requirements in the Law, the Israelites tended to despise and condemn the Gentiles for being uncircumcised and ignorant. Indeed it would only be in the gospel that Jew and Gentile would become reconciled to each other, as Paul declares in Ephesians 2:11–22. Instead of being divided by the fact that one race possessed the Law and all the others were ignorant of it, people of all nations are reconciled in their common possession of the gospel. We cannot be reconciled to God without being reconciled to all who believe in God through Christ. In times of war Christians have always found it hard to see as enemies those who are their friends in the gospel.

B. THE LAW WAS TEMPORARY AND THE GOSPEL IS ETERNAL.

This should be abundantly clear from the first point, but it is spelt out in a number of places. In Ephesians 2:14–17, Paul writes of the great work of reconciling sinners to God, a work which is for Gentile as well as Jewish sinners: both find peace with God through the same Saviour. In this way they are reconciled not only to God but to each other. This means that the Law which distinguished Israel from the Gentiles (see point 1 above) was redundant.

> *Christ destroyed the barrier, the dividing wall of hostility, by abolishing in his flesh the law with its commands and regulations* (Eph. 2:15).

Some say this refers to the ceremonial Law, but where does Paul say this? He specifies *commandments*, the term used for the moral stipulations rather than ceremonial directions. This does not mean morality is abolished, for, as shown in Chapter 2, morality predates Sinai and is forever. It applies to the legislation which constituted the covenant between God and Israel. Colossians 2:14 makes the same point:

> [Christ] *cancelled the written code, with its regulations, that was against us and stood opposed to us; he took it away, nailing it to the cross.*

In Galatians 3:19 Paul says that

> *The law was added [to the original promise to Abraham] until the seed to whom the promise referred had come,*

after which it ceased to be in force. Similarly in Galatians 3:24

> *the law was put in charge until Christ came, that we might be justified by faith. Now that faith has come we are no longer under a guardian* (ESV)

The word *until* is the Greek word *EIS* which does not mean *to lead us to*, something Paul never wrote, but which has been added by translators. This has altered the meaning, which is that the Law was in charge **until** Christ came. It was this mistranslation that led the Reformers to speak of the *usus pedagogues'* of the Law, the idea that the Law convicts us of sin and thus leads us to Christ. The ESV rightly translates it *until*. Paul is speaking here, not of personal experience, but salvation history. During the old covenant period salvation in its fullness still lay ahead. It corresponded to childhood in which the full enjoyment of family life and relationships is still to come. Paul is saying that, with the arrival of Messiah and the completion of his work of salvation, people can enter fully into the privileges of the children of God.

The letter to the Hebrews shows how Christ has taken over the work of high priest and become our intercessor before God, thus dispensing with the need for human priests: Heb. 4:14–5:11. The writer then goes on to say that

> *When there is a change of priesthood there must also be a change of law* (Heb. 7:12).

Unlike the priests under the Law Jesus has a "permanent priesthood" (Heb. 7:24), and has become the "guarantee of a better covenant" (Heb. 7:22). So with the arrival of his kingdom there is a new covenant, a new priesthood and a new law. Unlike the old, this is permanent, that is, it will last through this present age until his return. The gospel is eternal (Rev. 6:14).

This was demonstrated long before Christ came, in fact, during the time when the Law was being issued. When Moses came down from the mountain his face shone. Moses veiled his face because the Israelites could not bear to look at it. But the glory faded, so that the veil then prevented them from seeing that happening! In 2 Corinthians 3:7–18 Paul makes the point that the fading of the glory indicated that the glory of the Law was likewise impermanent and is outshone by the ministry of the Spirit. Jews who remain committed to the old covenant now have the veil over their hearts, which prevents them from seeing that the Law of the old covenant has passed away. Only Christ can remove that veil.

C. THE LAW WAS WRITTEN ON STONE TABLETS, THE GOSPEL ON THE HEART.

The passage referred to above, which speaks of the fading glory of the Law (2 Cor. 3) also makes this point: Paul speaks of the Corinthian Christians as

> *a letter from Christ, written not with ink but with the Spirit of the living God, not on tablets of stone but on tablets of human hearts* (2 Cor. 3:3)

Jeremiah predicted this (Jer. 31:33), which is quoted by Hebrews 10:14:

> This is the covenant I will make with them after that time, says the Lord: I will put my laws in their hearts and write them on their minds.

What is the significance of this? It does not mean that the Law is not spiritual. David famously said: "you desire truth in the inward parts" (Psalm 51:6), and Paul made the categorical statement "the law is spiritual" (Rom. 7:14), adding "in my inner being I delight in the law of God" (Rom. 7:21). E.F. Kevan wrote:

> The spiritual nature of the demands of the Law of God is a corollary of its nature as the transcript of the holy character of God. The Law's demands are inward, touching motive and desire, and are not concerned solely with outward action.[43]

Neither does it mean that those saved in Christ are more *willing* to obey God than those who came before. The *heart* does not mean the *will* or the emotions, but refers more to the understanding. Now that the Spirit has come to enlighten us we have a much greater understanding of the Word of God (Luke 24:45, 1 Cor. 2:12). Because we do not slavishly follow the rules given to Israel does not mean we jettison them, but that we understand their abiding meaning.

What it does mean is that under the new covenant of Christ's kingdom the motivation to obey God comes not from outside but from inside. The Israelite was compelled by something external, a written command carrying with it the sanction of physical punishment—beating, stoning, fining or even killing. But the believer in Christ is motivated from within, from his heart. The person who is righteous (justified) in Christ knows from within him what pleases or

---

[43] Kevan, *Grace of Law* 63.

displeases Christ; he does not need a book of rules. Jerome asked: "What need has the law to say to a righteous man 'Thou shalt not kill,' when it is not permitted to him even to be angry?" Chrysostom wrote:

> A righteous man does not need the law, nor does he require teaching or admonishing, indeed he disdains to be warned of it, and he does not want to stay to learn of it. As therefore a musician or grammarian, who has these arts within him, scorns the idea of consulting the rules or the grammar, so does a righteous man.[44]

To put it another way, he obeys Christ because he wants to, and he wants to because he loves him. "Let God give what he commands, and command what he wills" (Augustine). This does not mean there was no love under the old covenant. The writer of Psalm 119 expresses his love for the Law several times and in strong terms. But how many were like him? Asaph challenges the people thus:

> *What right have you to recite my laws or take my covenant on your lips? You hate instruction and cast my words behind you* (Psalm 50:15–16).

Not much love there!

D. THE LAW DECLARES THE HOLY WILL OF GOD AND THE GOSPEL ESTABLISHES IT.

God is holy and righteous and expects his creature man to be like him since he made him in his likeness. Unfallen man did this naturally, but through the fall man lost not only the ability and will to live righteously, but even the knowledge of just what that meant. While he retained a conscience which gave some basic awareness of right and wrong, this became confused and subject to evil influences, so that it might even reverse the two. There are those who "call evil good and good evil" (Isaiah 5:20). God made a full

---

[44] Quoted by E.F. Kevan, *The Moral Law*, 35.

declaration of what is right and wrong in the Sinai Law (Rom. 7:12). By obeying this Law his people Israel could experience the favour of God, enjoy his blessings and avoid his judgments.

When the gospel came along, it revealed a different way of achieving this goal. For in fact no one did come to righteousness and life through the Law, for:

> *by observing the law no one will be justified* (Gal. 2:16, see also Rom. 3:20).

Again,

> *The law was powerless in that it was weakened by the sinful nature. But what the law was powerless to do...God did by sending his own Son in the likeness of sinful man to be a sin offering. And so he condemned sin in sinful man, in order that the righteous requirements of the law might be fully met in us who do not live according to the sinful nature but according to the Spirit* (Rom. 8:3-4).

Though the way of the Gospel is different from the way of the Law, it is not **against** the law. When Paul wrote in Romans 3:28 "that a man is justified by faith apart from observing the law" he posed the question some were raising:

> *Do we then nullify the law by this faith? He answered: not at all, rather we uphold the law* (Rom. 3:31).

Paul's teaching on the Law sometimes sounds confusing, even contradictory. In this chapter (Rom. 3) he has been rejecting the Law as the way to righteousness in favour of the way of faith in Christ (Rom. 3:20–23). Yet he ends by saying that the way of faith-righteousness does not "nullify the law" but rather "upholds" it. This is explained by ascertaining which of the five meanings of *law* he is referring to. It is clear that he means the eternal moral law rather than the Sinai code. Righteousness by faith in Christ is in complete accord with God's eternal holy will. The Sinai code is one expression of that and formed the covenant between

God and Israel. This means that in essence the Sinai Law was upheld in the Gospel, in the sense that its intention of revealing God's holiness and requiring holiness from his people is upheld. Dr Kevan is helpful on this point:

> The Law is established by the Gospel in three ways. Firstly, in respect of its penalties: this aspect was established in Christ, who satisfied the justice of God. Secondly, in respect of its requirement of perfect obedience: this also was fulfilled in Christ. Thirdly, and what seems to be Paul's chief purpose in this passage, the Law is established by the Gospel because the believer obtains grace in some measure to fulfil the Law.[45]

It may be objected that Paul cannot be changing the meaning of *Law* from one thing—Sinai—at the beginning of Romans 3:31, to another thing—the eternal moral law—at the end. However, since Sinai was one expression of that law, there is no real difficulty.

There are two ways in particular by which the Gospel establishes the holy will of God, expressed in the Law.

1. *Its demands were fully met by Christ.* He perfectly obeyed the Law: actively, by carrying out all its precepts to the letter, and passively, by bearing its threatened punishments, its curse, by hanging on a tree. Since he had no sins of his own to be punished, he suffered vicariously so that the punishment of our sins may be placed on him and his righteousness imputed to us. By laying sins on his Son, God "demonstrated his justice" (Rom. 3:25). In this way the gospel "reveals the righteousness of God" (Rom. 1:17).

2. *It is the Holy Spirit who imparts the faith which receives Christ's atonement and imputed righteousness.* The Spirit then continues his ministry throughout our lives in the work of sanctification, by which we become more and

---

[45] Kevan, *The Moral Law*, 82.

more conformed to the likeness of Christ. The ethical demands of Christ and the apostles are not less than those of the Law; rather they exceed it, for they cover thoughts, feelings and intentions, as well as actions. In this way what Paul wrote in Romans 8:3–4 is carried out. So the likeness of God is seen far more in Christians than it ever was in those who followed the Sinai code!

E. THE LAW CONDEMNS, THE GOSPEL JUSTIFIES.

The Law never succeeded in achieving salvation from sin and judgment, as has just been mentioned:

If a law had been given that could impart life, then righteousness would certainly have come by the law (Gal. 3:21).

Then why did God say in Deuteronomy 4:1 and again in Deuteronomy 8:1 that if Israel followed the Laws God gave them they would live? Similarly in Leviticus 18:5: "the man who obeys them will live by them" (quoted by Paul in Rom. 10:5). The *life* promised there is not eternal life, but life in the land, as those chapters make clear. The enjoyment of the land of promise was dependent on obedience to the Law. When they ceased obeying they were expelled from the land.

These statements about life therefore refer to Israel's enjoyment of their covenant with God which promised them a land. Those who would enjoy its blessings must keep its conditions. This was *life* to the Israelite. Similarly, the rich young ruler in the gospels, although he enquired about eternal life (Matt. 19:16–30), was clearly thinking as an Israelite about enjoying life in the promised land forever, rather than salvation from sin. Jesus addressed him in the terms in which he was thinking and so referred to the terms of the covenant of Sinai. Nevertheless there is a connection between this and the Abrahamic covenant: God made a covenant with Abraham but then told him he must "walk before me and be blameless" (Gen. 17:1). The same is true for the Christian, as brought out in James 2:14–26, where he tells us the Christian must show his faith by his works; Christians under the new covenant are also to "walk before God and be blameless." Our difference from the Israelite is that we have another rule—the law of Christ rather than that of Moses.

However, the Law, rather than giving life, brought death. Paul who, as a Jew, had looked for life through the Law

> *... found that the very commandment that was intended to bring life actually brought death* (Rom. 7:10).

Of this he made a universal principle in Galatians 3:10:

> *All who rely on observing the law are under the curse, for it is written, "Cursed is everyone who does not continue to do everything written in the book of the law."*

The curse is the curse of condemnation for sin:

> *Judgment followed one sin and brought condemnation* (Rom. 5:16).

The Law's demands are total and absolute, as James says in James 2:10–11:

> *For whoever keeps the whole law and yet stumbles at just one point is guilty of breaking all of it.*

There is no escape from its condemnation; appealing to your obedience to one Law does not excuse you from breaking another. The Law covenant was conditional on the people's obedience, as is set forth in Deuteronomy 28. The Gospel, however, is conditional on Christ's obedience, which has been fulfilled. Therefore by the Gospel

> *Through him everyone who believes is justified from everything you could not be justified from by the law of Moses* (Acts 13:39).

Justification through faith in Christ releases from condemnation:

There is no condemnation for those who are in Christ Jesus (Rom. 8:1).

This teaching is, of course, the theme of the first eight chapters of Romans.

F. THE LAW HOLDS US IN BONDAGE, THE GOSPEL SETS US FREE.

When Paul was seeking to persuade the Galatians not to be circumcised because it would put them back under the Law, he used the argument that this would be slavery. As Gentiles they were brought up in slavery "to those who by nature are not gods" (Gal. 4:8). There was no pleasure in serving those gods, who made excessive demands on them and denied them the essentials of life if they refused to meet these demands. Coming to the God of the Bible had released them from their obligation to these gods. Now if they submitted themselves to the law, they would be "enslaved...all over again" (Gal. 4:9).

He compares the age of the Law to childhood (Gal. 3:23 - 4:3. See on pages 77 and 118). Jews before Christ were like children in Roman families who were brought up with the children of the household slaves, and "subject to guardians and trustees until the time set by the father" (Gal. 4:2). This means the time when they would cease to be under those who were "put in charge of them" (Gal. 3:24) and come directly under the supervision of the father, have free access to him, enjoy his love and be given greater freedom and responsibility, which Paul calls "the full rights of sons" (Gal. 4:5). In fact, he goes further and speaks of sinners under the Law as being its "prisoners, locked up until faith should be revealed" (Gal. 3:23).

For, since they had not yet come to know Christ intimately, they were like children, whose weakness could not yet bear the full knowledge of heavenly things.[46]

The Mosaic administration as a legal administration related to Israel as little children who did not quite understand the greatness and goodness of God's grace: Deut. 8:5, 32:7–15, Hosea 11:1, cf., Gal. 4:1–7, 21–31.[47]

This promotion from slavery to sonship corresponds to the coming of Christ and his being received by believers:

> *But when the time had fully come, God sent his Son, born of a woman, born under law, to redeem* [set free] *those under the law, that we might receive the full rights of sons* (Gal. 4:4–5).

For the believer this right is the right of direct access to the Father, which is the fruit of our justification through faith (Rom. 5:1–2). This brings us into the Father's love, which he

> *... has poured out ... into our hearts by the Holy Spirit, whom he has given us* (Rom 5:5).

We are then led by the Spirit because we are "sons of God" (Rom. 8:14). Being "led by the Spirit (we) are not under law" (Gal. 5:18). This is what James is talking about when he speaks of "the perfect law that gives freedom" (James 1:25). This 'perfect law' is the gospel and it is perfect because it does what the Sinai Law could not do—gives freedom from sin. The Law restrains from excessive sin, it keeps man under some kind of control and prevents the world from falling apart. To those who take it seriously this involves striving against the pull of the flesh and the pressure of the world. But the gospel is simply and freely received, that is, Christ, who is its subject, is personally welcomed. He does not have to be hunted high and low (Rom. 10:1–7) for he is here in the word of the gospel, and has but to be received and acknowledged for us to be saved and justified (Rom. 10:8–13). We can see from all of this why

---

[46] Calvin, *Institutes*, II.vii.2.

[47] W.A.van Gemeren, *Five Views of Law and Gospel*, 29.

Paul gloried in being "called to be an apostle, set apart for the gospel of God" (Rom. 1:1). He had been a zealous preacher of the Law until the call came. The glory of his old calling, such as it was, became eclipsed by the greater glory of his new calling.

This raises the whole subject of liberty, to which we now turn.

CHAPTER 8
LAW AND LIBERTY

Isaiah predicted that when Christ came, he would among other things "proclaim freedom to the captives and release from darkness the prisoners" (Isaiah 61:1). When Jesus began his ministry, he took this verse as his text for his first sermon, preached in the synagogue at Nazareth (Luke 4:18). Later he put this in his own words in John 8:31–36:

If the Son sets you free you will be free indeed (John 8:36).

A. THE FREEDOM BROUGHT BY CHRIST

It is fairly well known and generally agreed that Christ set his believing people free from sin—not only its guilt and punishment but also its dominion and bondage; see, for example, Romans. 6:6–7, 11–14, 17–18, 7:24–25a, 1 John 3:5–6, 17–18. What is not so well known and agreed upon is that he also set us free from bondage to **Law.** In Romans 6:14 Paul declares

You are not under law but under grace.

By *under* he meant under the dominion or power of the Law. In other words you who are in Christ are not only free from sin but from the Law. Some say this means we are not under the Law for justification. However, the subject of Romans 6 is not justification but sanctification. Paul used the same expression in Romans 3:19:

*Now we know that, whatever the law says, it says to those who are **under the law**...* (emphasis mine).

In that chapter Paul was seeking to convict Jews that they are as sinful before God as Gentiles. Gentiles who "do not have the law" (Rom. 2:14) are sinners against nature and conscience. But Jews do not only *have the law*; they are *under*

it: it is given to control their behaviour; it is like a master or
king whom they are under, whom they are obliged to obey.
As we have seen, it constitutes their covenant with God to
which they are committed. Believers in Christ, however,
whether Jews or Gentiles, are not in that covenant of law
declared at Sinai. They are in covenant with Christ who is
their master. Their obligation is to him, not to the Law of
Moses.

Paul developed this in Romans 7:1–6 by using the
analogy of marriage. In Galatians 5:1, referring to the Law
(to which the Galatians had returned) he wrote:

> *It is for freedom that Christ has set us free. Stand, then, and do
> not let yourselves be burdened again by a yoke of slavery.*

He also used the expression *died* or *dead to the law* in
Romans 7:4, where he likens the Law to the dead husband of
a woman–she is no longer under his authority. This
therefore means that, **as far as believers are concerned, the
Sinai Law is dead.** He says something similar in Galatians 2
when he is urging the newly-converted Gentiles and former
Jews not to go along with the teaching of the Judaizers from
Jerusalem who were saying that they must not only believe
in Christ but be circumcised and go on to observe the Law of
Moses. As in Romans 7 he uses himself as an example:

> *For through the law I died to the law so that I might live to God*
> (Gal. 2:19).

If this is too strong and suggests we are free from all law,
including the eternal moral law, then it can mean, not that
the Law itself is dead but that its power over us is dead. He
is speaking, not of the eternal moral law, but the Law of
Moses. Nor is he referring to it as a covenant of works or a
means of justification, but as a *custodian* or *supervisor*, in the
sense in which this word is used in Galatians 3:23–25.

All this is very clear; the question is what did he mean by it? To answer this we must return to our original principle of the precise meaning of *law* in this context. As usual, Paul is speaking of the Law of Moses, the code of Sinai. Clearly he is not speaking of the moral law in the sense of the absolute standards of morality derived from the nature of God himself and of man made in his image, as described in Chapter 1. In 1 Corinthians 9:21, in the process of describing his freedom from the Mosaic Law, Paul hastens to correct any suggestion that he is advocating antinomianism by inserting the words "I am not free from God's law," clearly distinguishing God's law from Moses' Law, from which he says he *is* free.

Having clarified that, we may now take note of the ways in which Christ has set us free from the Law (of Moses).

(a) As a means of righteousness: The Jew made the mistake of thinking he could attain righteousness by carefully observing Law:

> Since they did not know the righteousness that comes from God, and sought to establish their own, they did not submit to God's righteousness (Rom. 10:3).

That they failed to do so Paul has already stated in Romans 3 where, after quoting several passages which specify certain sins of the Jews, he draws his conclusion in verses 19–20:

> Now we know that whatever the law says it says to those who are under the law, so that every mouth may be silenced and the whole world held accountable to God. Therefore no one will be held righteous in his sight by observing the law, rather, through the law we become conscious of sin (Rom. 3:19–20).

The Law he has quoted is the Law given to Israel; it is they who are "under the law." They knew it and had consented to it, so that they had no excuse. The mouth of every Jew was stopped by their knowledge of and consent to the Law.

It held them all accountable. It was therefore of no use their appealing to their knowledge of the Law for justification in the sight of God. All they could get from it was the knowledge that they were in a state of sin.

Over against this he affirmed the true way of righteousness brought by Christ in Romans 3:21–22, 10:4. The Jews therefore should cease to struggle for righteousness by obeying the Law and take hold of that provided by Christ. When they do that they will find themselves free from the Law.

> Therefore, the consciences of believers, in seeking assurance of their justification before God, should rise above and advance beyond the law, forgetting all law-righteousness.[48]

(b) As a provoker of sin: When Paul came under conviction of sin, he found things were even worse than he had thought. Not only was the Law no road to righteousness, but it even provoked him to sin more. The more he knew about what he should or should not do the more he found himself doing what he should not—Romans 7:7–11! This was part of that "body of death" from which Christ set him free.

(c) As an executioner: As part of the above process Paul spoke of the Law slaying him: Romans 7:9–11. This is probably the same as what he meant by "the curse of the law" in Galatians 3:13. The curse is the curse of death. For Christ this meant crucifixion. For us it means death— spiritual, physical and eternal. Paul then adds

> Christ has redeemed us from the curse of the law by becoming a curse for us, for it is written "Cursed is everyone who is hung on a tree."

Instead of the curse we now have a blessing (Gal. 3:14)— none other than the blessing given to Abraham, that is righteousness through faith (cf. Gen. 15:6).

---

[48] Calvin, *Institutes,* III.ix.2.

(d) As an obligation: Believers under the new covenant are obliged to obey God and do his will, but not by keeping the Law of Moses, except where it corresponds to eternal or natural law or the precepts of Christ. This is more controversial and will not command the same agreement as the first three points. However, following the statements just considered in Galatians 3:13–14, Paul argues that the blessing promised to Abraham was unaffected by the giving of the law 430 years later (Gal. 3:15–18). He also says that the blessing came with Christ (Gal. 3:16) which means the period of the law was temporary—"until Christ came."

The Law was not redemptive, it was not the way to righteousness with God; it was a holding operation, restraining sin and preserving the promise of Messiah's kingdom and the new covenant "until Christ came" to deliver us from the Law. So he ends that section by saying

Now that faith has come we are no longer under the supervision of the law (Gal. 3:25).

In chapter 5 he discusses slavery to the law, as already mentioned. To submit to circumcision, to which the Pharisaic party was pushing them, would be to put themselves under an obligation to "the whole law" (Gal. 5:3). Gentile believers need not be circumcised because they are free from this obligation, as are Jews on coming to faith in Christ.

It has to be remembered that, as already stated, he is using the term *law* to apply to the Law of Moses, not the eternal moral law of God which is always in force. In fact, it was because we were in breach of it that Christ came and died, so that we might be both forgiven our sins against it and be given the will and power to keep it. These two points are very clear from Romans 8:3–4. These verses justify his claim in Romans 8:2 that through Jesus Christ "the law of

the Spirit of life set me free from the law of sin and death,"
that is, the Law that defines sin and condemns the sinner.

It is important to distinguish this teaching from what is
known as antinomianism. Antinomianism is a version of
Christianity which has reared its ugly head from time to
time in the history of the church.

First came the teaching Paul found himself up against in
Rome—since salvation is through grace and not the works of
the Law (in fact, the more sin abounds the more grace
abounds) then it is quite all right to go on sinning (Rom. 6:1).

In Ephesus a teaching sprang up associated with a certain
Nicolas, which Christ in his letter to that church through
John said he 'hated' (Rev. 2:6). This is referred to more
extensively in the letter to Pergamum (Rev. 2:14–15), where
it is connected with what is called "the teaching of Balaam:"
that idolatry and immorality are acceptable in Christians.
This seems to have developed into the Gnosticism associated
with the churches of Asia Minor, which taught quite
blatantly that the body is evil but the spirit, since it is
separated from the body or is even unreal, is unaffected by
it. This gave rise to false views of Christ's incarnation and
atonement, with which John contended in his first letter,
which is generally associated with Ephesus.

Soon after the close of the New Testament age, in about
160 AD, came Marcion who saw the Law as belonging to the
Old Testament age and therefore finished with the dawn of
the Gospel age. Marcion, therefore, did not even have to
argue a case for a believer's freedom from the Law because
it became obsolete from the end of the OT age.

The vogue for mysticism which developed in the
mediaeval church made spiritual experience the be-all and
end-all of Christianity and tended to breed an indifference to
moral behaviour.

During the Reformation, Luther contended against it in the teaching of Agricola and a group called Flacians who denied that good works had any place in the Christian life. In Geneva, a sect called the Libertines gave Calvin no end of grief, since they stretched Christian liberty to such an extent that it had no qualifications or conditions, a state which we would call permissive.

In the seventeenth century Puritan age some, such as Tobias Crisp, John Saltmarsh and John Eaton, put such an emphasis on grace that they left little or no room for ethical teaching or requirements. Their personal conduct was above reproach, far from that of the Libertines, and seems quite out of keeping with their teaching. Their type of antinomianism seems to have been purely theoretical, based on logic rather than Scripture. However, their emphasis greatly weakened the call of the gospel for repentance and faith, which to them sounded more like works than grace, or works of which man was incapable.

The last major advocate of this view was probably J.N. Darby, founder of Brethrenism, although he arrived at it by a very different route from that of the seventeenth century divines. In his case it was based on dispensational teachings, which held that whole sections of Scripture do not apply in the present age. The Law belonged to Israel; the present age is the Church age or the Gospel age and the Law is irrelevant to it. However, it will be re-instated after Israel's restoration to their land, and this will include all the ceremonies of the Law.

A fuller survey of antinomianism down the ages can be found in E.F. Kevan's *The Grace of Law* pages 22–28 and 31–36,[49] and in *No Holiness, No Heaven* by Richard Alderson,[50]

---

[49] E.F. Kevan, *The Grace of Law* (London: Carey Kingsgate Press, 1964).

[50] Publisher not known.

who also includes contemporary authors such as R.T. Kendall and Gerald Coates. The book was written before works on New Covenant Theology began to appear.

It is strange that all these teachings started from different places and took different routes, yet ended up with a similar conclusion—that the Law does not apply to believers.

The author of this work has tried to heed these warnings from history and to avoid going down any of these roads. His approach to the question of whether a Christian is "under the law" or in what sense "Christ is the end of the law" is not so much to discuss the words *under* and *end* as to examine what is meant by L*aw*. It is from the definition of that term that the position taken here is derived.

B. HOW THIS FREEDOM IS ATTAINED.

We do not free ourselves from sin and the Law, we have to *be freed*. Such is our bondage; only God himself can release us. It was he who gave us into the hands of these masters, and it must be he who sets us free from them. This he does through Christ and the Spirit.

1) The Work of Christ

- Christ set us free from *sin* by suffering its punishment for us:

You see, at just the right time, when we were still powerless, Christ died for the ungodly. Very rarely will anyone die for a righteous man, though for a good man someone might possibly die. But God demonstrates his own love for us in this: while we were still sinners, Christ died for us (Rom. 5:6–8).

God made him who had no sin to be sin for us, so that in him we might become the righteousness of God (2 Cor. 5:21).

He himself bore our sins in his body on the tree, so that we might die to sins and live for righteousness; by his wounds you have been healed (1 Pet. 2:24).

For Christ died for sins once for all, to bring you to God (1 Pet. 3:18).

- Christ set us free from *the Law* by: a) fulfilling its demands for us:

Let it be so now; it is proper for us to do this to fulfill all righteousness (Matt. 3:15).

Do not think that I have come to abolish the Law or the Prophets; I have not come to abolish them but to fulfill them (Matt. 5:17).

What the law was powerless to do in that it was weakened by the sinful nature, God did by sending his own Son in the likeness of sinful man to be a sin offering. And so he condemned sin in sinful man, in order that the righteous requirements of the law might be fully met in us, who do not live according to the sinful nature but according to the Spirit (Rom. 8:3–4).

... when Christ came into the world, he said:
"Sacrifice and offering you did not desire,
but a body you prepared for me;
with burnt offerings and sin offerings you were not pleased.

Then I said, 'Here I am—it is written about me in the scroll—

I have come to do your will, O God'."

First he said, "Sacrifices and offerings, burnt offerings and sin offerings you did not desire, nor were you pleased with them" (although the law required them to be made). Then he said, "Here I am, I have come to do your will." He sets aside the first to establish the second. And by that will, we have been made holy through the sacrifice of the body of Jesus Christ once for all (Heb. 10:5–10).

b) bearing its curse for us:

Christ redeemed us from the curse of the law by becoming a curse for us, for it is written, "Cursed is everyone who is hung on a tree" (Gal. 3:13).

Paul encourages those who have come to know and enjoy this freedom to "stand firm" in it and not allow themselves to be dragged back into slavery (Gal. 5:1). How do we do this and ensure we enjoy this freedom? For this we need the Spirit:

> *The law of the Spirit of life in Christ Jesus has set me free from the law of sin and death* (Rom. 8:2).

(2) The Work of the Spirit

The Spirit's work is not, like Christ's, *for us*, but *in us*. By the Spirit we are "born again" (John 3:3, 5, Titus 3:5), recreated, "made new in our minds" (Eph. 4:23). "Strengthened with power through the Spirit in our inner being" (Eph. 3:18), and "renewed in the image of our Creator" (Col. 3:10). In this way the promise of the new covenant is fulfilled: "I will put my law in their minds and write it on their hearts" (Jer. 31:33). This is a work of cleansing from the old impure thoughts and feelings, as foretold by Ezekiel:

> *I will sprinkle clean water upon you and you will be clean; I will cleanse you from all your impurities and all your idols. I will give you a new heart and put a new spirit in you; I will remove from you your heart of stone and give you a heart of flesh* (Ezek. 36:25–26).

The result of this will be:

> *I will put my Spirit in you and move you to follow my decrees and be careful to keep my laws* (Ezek. 36:27).

"Writing the law on the heart" means it is obeyed willingly not forcibly.

> The second part of Christian freedom is that consciences obey the law, not as if constrained by the necessity of the law, but that, free from the law's yoke, they willingly obey God's will.[51]

There is a greater desire for *knowledge* of the whole will of God (Col. 3:10) and a desire to *obey* it. It is kept out of love for God and a reverent *fear* towards him: 2 Corinthians 7:1, 1

---

[51] Calvin, *Institutes*, III.xix.4.

Peter 1:17. This fear is not the same as being afraid of God, that is, of his judgment, but an attitude of awe and wonder springing from this greater knowledge of him that comes through regeneration; it draws us to him rather than drives us from him. So it in no way inhibits freedom but rather enhances it, for it sets us free from bondage to fleshly passions, enabling us to walk with him.

Although Jeremiah speaks of the new covenant as "the *law* written on the heart," the prophecy is not fulfilled by our keeping the law of Moses with its numerous and detailed restrictions and its imposition of an elaborate system of ceremonies (Col. 2:20–23). It is fulfilled in keeping the law of the new covenant, that is, the law of Christ (1 Cor. 9:21). Paul is not "*under* the law" but neither is he "*without* law," for he is "under law" (or "within the law") to Christ, that is, he is subject to Christ's lordship and must obey his commands. Paul may have had Jeremiah's words in mind when he wrote that Christians are "a letter from Christ...written not with ink but with the Spirit of the living God, not in tables of stone but in tables of human hearts" (2 Cor. 3:3). The glory of the old covenant is fading away and the glory of the new covenant is shining, a covenant not of law but of the Spirit. If the work of the Spirit had been to make us remember the Sinai code and keep it meticulously, this would scarcely be freedom. We are "the living letter of Christ" not the code of Sinai on legs! What does Christ teach us? In what code of behaviour do the apostles instruct us? It is these we love, to these we freely commit ourselves. Romans 8:1–4 shows that the way of faith in Christ succeeds where the Law fails, and it succeeds by walking in the Spirit and in love.

C. THE USES TO WHICH THIS FREEDOM IS PUT

Not only does this freedom enable us to obey God willingly and acceptably, but it has other functions.

(1) In worship. We are released from prescribed ceremonies and the observance of days. Under the old covenant there were many rituals and sacrifices, some of which were obligatory: Passover, Pentecost, Tabernacles and the Day of Atonement. Israelites were to assemble at Jerusalem to participate in these, for no other altars were permitted. As well as these special festivals, there was a monthly observation—the new moon–and the weekly Sabbath, which was strictly regulated and no work was permitted. There were also daily morning and evening sacrifices, although only priests were obliged to attend these.

Under the new covenant none of these regulations applies (Col. 2:11-23). The entrance into the old covenant for an Israelite was circumcision on the eighth day. That committed him to the whole Law, including its ceremonies. In Colossians 2:11 Paul says that we Christians have been circumcised "not by the hands of men but with the circumcision done by Christ," which he describes as "putting off the sinful nature," in other words regeneration in Christ (Col. 2:13–15). Of this, baptism is an even better illustration than circumcision, as Paul says:

> Buried with him in baptism and raised with him through the power of God who raised him from the dead (Col. 2:12).

Along with the removal of the requirement of circumcision go all the other ceremonial obligations:

> Therefore do not let anyone judge you by what you eat or drink, or with regard to a religious festival, a new moon celebration or a Sabbath day. These are a shadow of the things that were to come; the reality, however, is found in Christ (Col. 2:16, 17).

Does this mean there are no instructions about worship under the new covenant? There are, but they are broad and spiritual. In John 4:23–24 we are told that because "God is Spirit" his worshippers "must worship him in spirit and in truth." Our renewed nature, our spirit, goes out to him in awe and wonder, love and faith.

This of course is what the individual believer does, so what about corporate worship? For this the church is supplied with "psalms, hymns and spiritual songs" (Eph. 5:19), no doubt old and new, comprising the psalms of the Old Testament and songs and hymns composed by Christians, of which the New Testament gives some examples. That these are used by Christians meeting together is clear from the words *speak to one another* with psalms, hymns and spiritual songs." This also must not be done mechanically or as an obligation, but with a heart that "sings and makes music…to the Lord." For this it is necessary to be "filled with the Spirit" (Eph. 5:18), which brings us back to John 4:23–24. This is freedom in worship. The matter of the Sabbath, the Lord's Day or Sunday will be looked at in Chapter 9.

(2) In the enjoyment of the things of the earth. Israelites faced a number of restrictions on their use of earthly things. These principally applied to food, which was tightly regulated as to what was permissible and what was not. Some of these are still in force today for Jews. Meat has to be kosher, of the right kind, prepared by Jewish butchers and cooked in a certain way. Christ swept all this away with a stroke when he was in dispute with the Pharisees over what was clean and what was not. He stated that it was not what goes into the mouth that makes a man unclean but what comes out of his heart: Mark 7:14–22. When he said this, says Mark, "he declared all foods clean."

Paul also spoke against asceticism in Colossians 2:20–23. Then, in 1 Timothy 4:1–5 he made a virtually definitive statement on the matter when he said

Everything God created is good and nothing is to be rejected if it is received with thanksgiving.

Similarly he said in 1 Timothy 6:17

God richly provides us with everything for our enjoyment.

Calvin, while opposing the abuse of Christian freedom for gluttony and luxury, regarded created things as things indifferent, not controlled by laws. Although he has a reputation for austerity and even being against laughter, he wrote:

We have never been forbidden to laugh, or to be filled, or to join new possessions to old or ancestral ones, or to delight in musical harmony, or to drink wine.[52]

Peter is an example of one who was still under the Law in these matters until he was freed by a special revelation from God: Acts 10. But this was really to set him free from an even deeper prejudice—against Gentiles. Although he baptised Cornelius with water and the Spirit, he lapsed when in Antioch with Paul, and refused to eat with Gentiles, for which Paul had to take him to task: Galatians 2:11–21.

D. THE LIMITS OF FREEDOM

Christian freedom does not mean "do as you like without regard to anything or anyone." It has its boundaries. Conscience will help us recognise these, but it is not adequate. It can mislead us if it is not rightly instructed. It even leads some to commit murder. God is Lord of our conscience and he has defined the areas and limits of our freedom in his word, especially in the following ways.

1) Expediency.

"Everything is permissible for me"—but not everything is beneficial (1 Cor. 6:12).

---

[52] Calvin, *Institutes*, III.xix.9.

This is Paul's principle with regard to bodily things. What is permissible (not forbidden by the Law) may not be beneficial. He restates this in 1 Corinthians 10:23 in connection with the matter of eating food that had been sacrificed to idols, which was a big issue in the pagan society in which the first Christians lived. Since idols are not really gods, in fact not real in any sense, offering meat to them in no way affects the meat itself. But there may be weak Christians present who think it does. For their sake the stronger Christian should be willing to forego his freedom:

> Be careful, however, that the exercise of your freedom does not become a stumbling block to the weak (1 Cor. 8:9).

Hebrews 12:1 points out that it is not only *sins* that we should cast off but *hindrances*. When we exercise our freedom to eat or drink what we like, to read books or watch films, to indulge in activities or go to places, we should consider what effect this will have both on ourselves and others.

2) Commitment. We are not free to enter into relationships with unbelievers that may compromise our commitment to Christ, the gospel and the church: 2 Corinthians 6:14–7:1. This passage is usually applied to marriage, which is certainly included, but it goes beyond that to other commitments, such as those in the business world. Perhaps in the context the primary reference is to church membership, which is a kind of covenant relationship, and must therefore exclude unbelievers.

3) Addiction. Going back to 1 Corinthians 6:12, where Paul distinguishes what is permissible from what is beneficial, he adds "I will not be mastered by anything." Freedom can become bondage. I am free to drink alcohol but there is a danger of becoming addicted to it and therefore mastered by it. This applies to foods, to tobacco, to sex, to sports and many other things. "I can give it up whenever I like" has proved the road to disaster for many.

4) Love. Freedom can become self-indulgence. The best antidote to this is to consider the effect of our freedom on others, that is, to act in love:

> You, my brothers, were called to be free. But do not use your freedom to indulge the sinful nature; rather, serve one another in love (Gal. 5:13).

In the matter of freedom, as already mentioned, we must consider the Christian who has not yet discovered and entered into this glorious liberty, but is struggling with his conscience. Paul called such "one whose faith in weak" (Rom. 14:1) and warns us that if we flaunt our freedom before such a one we are no longer acting in love:

> If your brother is distressed because of what you eat, you are no longer acting in love. Do not by your eating destroy your brother for whom Christ died (Rom. 14:15).

Our freedom must be subordinated to love, which is after all the first law of Christ's kingdom (John 13:34).

> We must at all times seek after love and look toward the edification of our neighbour. "All things" he [Paul] says elsewhere, "are lawful to me, but not all things are helpful. All things are lawful, but not all things build up. Let no one seek his own good but another's" (1 Corinthians 10:23–24). Nothing is plainer than this rule, that we should use our freedom if it results in the edification of our neighbour. But if it does not help our neighbour we should forego it.[53]

We must be careful that "this brother for whom Christ died" is not 'destroyed by our knowledge.' We are not to "cause anyone to stumble, whether Jews, Greeks or the church of God" (1 Cor. 10:32).

---

[53] Calvin, *Institutes*, III.xix.12.

Even in Galatians where he is asserting Christian liberty as powerfully as ever he can, he qualifies it:

You, my brothers, were called to be free. But do not use your freedom to indulge the sinful nature; rather serve one another in love. The entire law is summed up in a single command: Love your neighbour as yourself (Gal. 5:13–14).

A little later, in Galatians 6:2, he speaks of acts of love as "fulfilling the law of Christ," that is, completely satisfying the demands of his law. How wisely does he at one and the same time maintain our freedom from Moses' law by appealing to the eternal law and qualify it by the law of love! He himself was a good example of this principle, in the matter of whether he should accept financial support from the churches he served. His principle was that he was free to do so, but restrained himself from exercising that freedom in the interests of the gospel. In 1 Corinthians 9, where he discusses this issue at length, he twice says "I have not used this (or these) right(s)" (1 Cor. 9:11, 15). This includes his right to take money, or to be accompanied in his travels by a wife, who would also need financial support. He also forewent this right: 1 Corinthians 9:5–6. In these days, when human rights are all the rage, we Christians have to be careful we do not claim rights which will harm our witness to the gospel.

What a balanced man Paul was! He never let his discovery of the wonderful truth of Christian freedom go to his head and knock him off his balance. Let us go and do likewise.

5) Government. Our freedom in Christ breaks down the barriers between sexes, nations, races and classes, according to Ephesians 2:14. This does not mean we completely ignore them. While we are still in the flesh and the world we remain what we always have been in terms of gender, race and nation. We are therefore bound to respect the rules and customs of our society.

> Therefore, in order that none of us may stumble on that score, let us first consider that there is a two-fold government in man: one aspect is spiritual, whereby our conscience is instructed in piety and in reverencing God; the second is political, whereby man is educated for the duties of humanity and citizenship that must be maintained among men.[54]

This particularly applies to the matter of government. The apostles nowhere teach that Christians are free to disobey the state. This is taught by Paul in Romans 13 and by Peter in 1 Peter 2:13–17. The only exception to this is where the state commands disobedience to God in a fundamental matter. To describe in detail what this means would take us beyond our present remit, but there are good examples in Acts 4:19–20, 5:29.

Let us follow Paul's example and teaching, enjoy our freedom to the fullest permissible extent, but be clear on where the boundaries lie. We have sufficient scope within these limits not to feel our freedom is being jeopardised.

---

[54] Calvin, *Institutes*, III.xix.15.

CHAPTER 9
SABBATH, LORD'S DAY OR SUNDAY?

This is probably the most controversial part of the whole subject. The tradition of remembering the Sabbath day, keeping the Lord's day or Sunday observance is so long and deeply rooted it is simply assumed to be right and any suggested alteration is fiercely challenged. Nothing requires a clearer or more open mind in approaching it than this subject.

The Names

The *Sabbath* is what OT Israel called the seventh day of the week. The noun is *SHABBATH*, first used in Exodus 16:23, 30 when Moses told the people not to gather manna on the seventh day but to eat what they had gathered on the sixth day because the seventh day is "a holy Sabbath to the Lord." Genesis 2:2–3 uses the verbal form *(Sabbathed)* when God, having completed his work of creation "rested from his work." Shortly after the gathering of the manna the requirement to rest on the seventh day is made compulsory in the fourth commandment (Ex. 20: 8–11).

"The first day of the week" is used several times in the NT. It was the day on which Christ rose from the dead (Matt. 28:1, Mark 16:2, Luke 24:1, John 20:1) and appeared to his disciples (John 20:19). On the first day of the following week he appeared again, this time with Thomas present (John 20:26). Subsequently it was the day on which Paul met with a number of Christians in Troas, broke bread (which is usually said to mean held the Lord's Supper) and preached

until midnight (Acts 20:7–12). It is suggested that Paul deliberately delayed his departure in order to be present to break bread on the first day of the week. They were careful to distinguish between Christian and Jewish worship and therefore did not refer to the first or Lord's day as the Sabbath, which only came about much later. In any case, some Jewish Christians continued to observe the seventh day Sabbath. Neither did they connect it with the fourth commandment until much later. When the Gentiles came into the church, observance of the seventh day Sabbath was dropped. This, together with the resurrection of Christ and his appearances is usually taken as the basis for Christians to meet together on the first rather than the seventh day.

"The Lord's day" is the day on which John, in prison on Patmos, was "in the Spirit" and had his vision of Christ (Rev. 1:10). He does not tell us on which day of the week this was, nor is there any mention of a Christian meeting—hardly likely in prison! However, it is the name that has become attached to the day on which Christians meet, the first day of the week. The expression *Lord's day* is used nowhere else in Scripture. The construction of the expression is interesting. In most English translations it appears as a genitive: "the Lord's day" or "the day of the Lord" (although that usually denotes a judgment day). But in Greek it is an adjective *TE KURIAKE HEMERA*. In secular Greek this means the Emperor's day or the imperial day, as it is translated in the *Nestle Interlinear New Testament.* What day that was is not clear; it may have been his birthday or coronation anniversary. But in either case or any other it would mean that **'the Lord' would not be Jesus Christ but Caesar!** To say "Caesar is Lord" was required of all within the Roman Empire. Was John imprisoned for refusing to say this? Was the imperial day Sunday, the day for the worship

of the sun? If so, it would certainly be the first day of the week.

The only other place where *KURIAKE* is used is 1 Corinthians 11:20—the Lord's Supper. It has been suggested that the Lord's day was the day on which the Lord's Supper was celebrated. However, it is more likely that the reason why *KURIAKE* was used in connection with the Lord's Supper is to distinguish it from pagan sacrificial meals. As regards the Lord's day, *KURIAKE* was probably used to distinguish it from *HEMERA KURIOS*, the day of the Lord, which in Scripture refers to a divine visitation in judgment, eventually used of the final day.

As to when and how Christian worship began to be held on the first day, the situation is not clear. It is not until the end of the second century that writers begin to refer to Sunday as "the Lord's day," and some may have meant Easter Day. Nor is it clear why the first day came to be chosen as the day for Christian worship. The usual explanation is that it was the day on which Jesus rose from the dead, though the connection may not have begun to be made until after the first day came into use. The first Christians continued to use the Sabbath, but when it became necessary to have a time for worship separate from the one used by the Jews, the day following the Sabbath was chosen. Ignatius, writing at the beginning of the second century, wrote of how Christian Jews "have given up keeping the Sabbath and order their lives by the Lord's day instead (the day when life first dawned for us, thanks to him and his death)..."[55] From the third century Origen and Eusebius both identify the Sabbath with the Lord's day. But in the fourth century Athanasius and Chrysostom distinguish the

---

[55] "Epistle to the Magnesians," *Early Christian Writings*, (Penguin Classics, 1968) 19.

Lord's day from the Sabbath, which they regard as not being obligatory for Christians. "If you keep the Sabbath day, why not be circumcised as well?" (Chrysostom).

John's use of the *Lord's day* in Revelation 1 is appropriate because the resurrection established Christ as Lord over all his foes and he will finally win the battles which form the subject of John's visions. Worshipping Christ on the Lord's day separates his worshippers from the worshippers of the beast.

Creation Ordinance

Genesis 2:1–3 are widely held to mean that, since God finished his work of creation on Day 6 and did not continue it on Day 7 but *rested*, we should emulate him by not working on that day. This is confirmed by Genesis 2:3: "God blessed the seventh day and made it holy." This would imply:

- That the observation of the Sabbath was obligatory from the beginning, not just from the giving of the commandments on Sinai.
- That it is binding on all men as descendants of Adam.

There are, however, problems with this view.

1. The noun *sabbath*, as already mentioned, is not used here, but it is the verbal form of the word: "God sabbathed from all his work." God did not call the seventh day "**the** sabbath" at this point. *Rested* is a little misleading. The meaning is *ceased*, that is, God did no more creating, because creation was complete. God did not need a rest, neither did Adam and Eve nor did the land. It does not mean God did no work after the sixth day, as Jesus said:

   My Father is always at work to this very day, and I too am working (John 5:17).

2. The sentence "there was evening and morning" used at the end of the work of the first six days is absent here. This suggests it is not a twenty-four hour day that is being referred to but something continuous. At some point in time God ceased creating, a state of things which has persisted since then. *The seventh day* is therefore still continuing. Those who regard the creation days as periods rather than twenty-four hour days will find it easier to accept this, but even those who take *the days* literally should be able to accept that the age of non-creation which began then is continuing still.

There is strong presumption in favour of the interpretation that this seventh day is not one that terminated at a certain point in history, but that the whole period of time subsequent to the end of the sixth day is the Sabbath alluded to in Genesis 2:2.[56]

There are two versions of the fourth commandment in the Old Testament: one in Exodus 20 and the other in Deuteronomy 5. The latter does not mention creation, but puts Israel's release from slavery in Egypt as the motivation for keeping the Sabbath. The words *as the Lord commanded*, therefore, refer to what he said at the Red Sea, not at creation. The question of the two versions is discussed fully by John Reisinger in *Tablets of Stone*, Chapter 3.[57]

It is not until the New Testament that we see the full meaning of this continuous Sabbath. Hebrews quotes both Genesis 2 (Heb. 4:4) and Psalm 95 (Heb. 4:3, 5 and Heb. 4:7). In the case of the latter (especially Heb. 4:11) the reference is not to a weekly day of rest but to the Promised Land. At

---

[56] John Murray, *Principles of Conduct* (London, Tyndale Press, 1957) 30.

[57] John G. Reisinger, *Tablets of Stone* (Frederick, MD, New Covenant Media, 2004) 27.

Kadesh Barnea the Israelites failed to believe God's promise to enter and conquer the land and that whole generation died without seeing it: Hebrews 4:6. This, however, does not exhaust the meaning of the promised rest: there is *another day* (Heb. 4:8)—a Sabbath day that remains (Heb. 4:9). This *rest* is the rest of ceasing from trying to enter the land, that is, the kingdom, by works, and instead seeking to do so by faith (Heb. 4:3). The rest, therefore, is both the present kingdom of Christ and the final heaven.

3. To speak of God as having "**blessed** the seventh day" is not the same as saying "he **commanded**" its observation. It can mean that, having created all things, his blessing rested on them, they were good and productive because he was caring for them. In other words it speaks of the work of creation as giving way to the work of providence, to which Christ was referring when he spoke of God *working* on the Sabbath in John 5:16–17. God's providential care for creation is his blessing on the continuing Sabbath.

4. But it also says he "made it holy," which suggests there was an obligation to use it not just for resting after a week's work but observing it in a particular way. This raises the question as to **when** he made it holy. If we consider **when** these words were written this should help clarify the matter. They were not written down at creation but by Moses sometime after God spoke to him on Sinai. During that forty day conference could it only have been the Law that God declared to him? It seems a long time just to hear and write down Exodus chapters 20 to 31. So it is not unreasonable to suggest that it was at this time that Moses wrote the whole of Genesis, Exodus and Leviticus. The important thing for the present discussion is that he wrote the account of creation at this time. So when he writes down Genesis

2:3 he has in mind the fourth commandment which he has just received and which is when God made the seventh day holy, not at creation. Moses' reference to Genesis 2:3 is to explain why the Sabbath is to be a cessation from work, that is, to remind the people of God's finished creation.

So Moses is not saying that God blessed and made holy the seventh day at creation but that he did it when he issued the commandment telling his people how to observe the day. There is no mention of humanity in Genesis 2:3. This is God's *day* to celebrate his finished creation. Its relevance for humanity did not come until later. A.T. Lincoln says that *therefore* in Exodus 20:11 ("therefore the Lord blessed the seventh day") is an example of *etiology*, when a present name or practice is explained on the basis of a previous event or story.[58] He had already begun to prepare the way for this when he gave the manna in Exodus 16. They were told to gather this every day, enough for each family. But on the sixth day they must gather enough for two days (Ex. 16:5). Later Moses explained the reason: "tomorrow is to be a day of rest, a holy Sabbath to the Lord" (Ex. 16:23). When the seventh day came he said "today is a Sabbath to the Lord" (Ex. 16:24) and added: "six days you are to gather it, but on the seventh day, the Sabbath, there will not be any" (Ex. 16:26). This is the first time the noun *Sabbath* is used and the people were clearly ignorant of it, for, in spite of all Moses said, some people "went out on the seventh day to gather it but found none" (Ex. 16:27). So Moses had to repeat the instructions in Exodus 16:28–29. If it was a 'creation ordinance' how was it that the people seemed to be totally ignorant of it?

---

[58] A.T. Lincoln, *From Sabbath to Lord's Day*, D.A. Carson, ed. (Eugene, OR, Wipf and Stock Publishers, 1999) 349.

What happened in Exodus 16 is made into a law in Exodus 20. This was when "God blessed the seventh day and made it holy," that is, it was to be a blessing to them, a time of rest for which God would provide, as the giving of the manna had shown, and also a glory to him, for it was to be made holy to him, and like him—to be separate, distinct from other days, a day which therefore honoured him.

So if the Sabbath was not a creation ordinance, what was it?

To answer this question we have to go back to what was said earlier of the Ten Commandments generally. They were the terms of God's **covenant** with Israel. Referring to the Ten Commandments which were to follow, Moses said:

> *Now if you obey me fully and keep my* **covenant***, then out of all nations you will be my treasured possession* (Ex. 19:5).

Referring back to Sinai before he repeated the Decalogue on the border of Canaan, Moses said:

> *The Lord our God made a* **covenant** *with us in Horeb* (Deut. 5:2).

The whole code was called "the Book of the **Covenant**" (Ex. 24:3–8). To break the law was therefore to break the **covenant:**

> *… if you reject my decrees and abhor my vows and fail to carry out all my commands and so violate my covenant …* (Lev. 26:15).

After the golden calf incident, when God made new tablets, Moses referred to this too as God's covenant: Exodus 34:28b.

The fourth commandment stood out from all the others as a *sign of the covenant:*

> *You must observe my Sabbaths. This will be a sign between me and you [that is, a sign of the covenant between them and God]. The Israelites are to observe the Sabbath, celebrating it for the generations to come as a lasting* **covenant** (Ex. 31:13, 16).

This appears to have been at least one reason why the Jews were held captive in Babylon for 70 years: the number corresponds to the number of years in which the land was not given its Sabbath rest (2 Chr. 36:21).

It was because God looked on the Sabbath as a covenant sign that he took its infringement so seriously when he said:

> *Whoever does any work on the Sabbath must be put to death.*

Why should it be a capital crime to do good on the Sabbath by working? Surely it does not compare in wickedness to murder, adultery and theft, or even to taking the Lord's name in vain. The only explanation is that observance of the Sabbath stood for observance of the whole code as God's covenant between them and him. To violate the Sabbath signified that the covenant itself was cast aside.

Since the gift of the land was part of the covenant (cf. Ex. 20:12)

> ...the land is included in the legislation for the Sabbath
> (Lev. 25:2). ...it must be treated with proper respect and care;
> every seventh year the land must be given a *rest* from seasonal
> cultivation.[59]

This especially applied in the fiftieth year, that is, after seven sevens of years (Lev. 25:8–12, 28).

The sign idea is also used by the prophets when seeking to convict the people of Israel of their rebelliousness against God and to encourage them to return to him, for example, in rehearsing the history of their unfaithfulness to the Lord and threatening them with dire punishments, Ezekiel says:

> *I gave them my Sabbaths as a sign between us...Yet the people of*
> *Israel rebelled against me at the desert. They did not follow my*
> *decrees but rejected my laws... and they utterly desecrated my*
> *Sabbaths* (Ezek. 20:12–13).

---

[59] Harold H.P. Dressler, *From Sabbath to Lord's Day*, D.A. Carson, ed. (Eugene, OR, Wipf and Stock Publishers, 1999) 31.

Just as violating the Sabbath brings down God's curse, so observing it brings his blessing:

> *If you keep your feet from breaking the Sabbath and from doing as you please on my holy day, if you call the Sabbath a delight and the Lord's holy day honourable, and if you honour it by not going your own way and not doing as you please or speaking idle words, then you will find your joy in the Lord and I will cause you to ride on the heights of the land and to feast on the inheritance of your father David* (Isaiah 58:13–14).

For the promise of blessing enshrined in God's covenant is even more prominent than the threat of cursing to law-breakers. God's covenant with Israel was to make them his *treasured possession* (Ex. 19:5). Because this was what they were he showered his blessings on them. One of them was the Sabbath itself:

> *The Lord blessed the seventh day and made it holy* (Ex. 20:11).

His Son confirmed this when he said 'The Sabbath was made for man' (Mark 2:27).

So it worked both ways: to keep the Sabbath was a sign of the enjoyment of the blessings of covenant relationship with God; to break it was to incur the curses of the covenant. This seems a better way of understanding the words of Genesis 2:2–3 than the *creation ordinance* idea. It could hardly be a sign of the covenant in Genesis 2, since the covenant had not been made then. There was no Israel with whom to make it.

The Fourth Commandment

Because it was a sign of the covenant the Sabbath had its own Law. It is this that explains its inclusion in a code of rules whose main orientation is moral. It is often said that, since the fourth commandment appears as part of the 'moral law,' it is therefore a moral matter. But how is it a matter of morality? How does it harm anyone else if I work on the Sabbath? Indeed, it can actually help them, which was what

Jesus himself taught in Mark 2:23–3:6. Surely the fourth commandment is religious rather than moral, that is, it concerns our relationship with God, it is kept in his honour as the Creator (Ex. 20:11) and Redeemer (Deut. 5:15). This applies to all the first four commandments, sometimes called "the first table of the Law." They are all to do with God himself, acknowledging him (I), worshipping him (II), using his name (III) and observing his day (IV). The term *ceremonial* is more appropriate than *moral*, though it is not the best one.

With this in mind, there are a number of points to consider.

1) *The command to* **remember***:* It is sometimes said that this word implies that the command was already in force when God spoke it and therefore it must date from creation. The Law is simply not to forget it. However, *remember* can be used prospectively as well as retrospectively: "now that I have given you this Law, remember to keep it." When Jesus said at the Last Supper "do this in remembrance of me" (Luke 22:19), he was not recalling something from the past but telling them what to do in the future. In days to come, after he has left them, they were to *remember* his death by doing as he did at the Last Supper. So what the Lord was telling Israel at Sinai was that from henceforth, especially when they were established in the Promised Land, they should remember to set aside this day. If it relates to the past at all it could be referring to Exodus 16 when they were told not to gather the manna on the Sabbath but to keep it holy. He is saying "remember to go on doing what you did then."

2) *The command to* **keep it holy***: Holy* means *set apart*, that is, from what is of man and the world, just as God is apart from and above human and worldly things. It was a sign of the covenant which said they belonged to the holy God and

were to live accordingly. They were special people and therefore special Laws applied to them. Setting aside the seventh day marked them off from others who did not keep that day special or if they had any special days they were in honour of false gods. How this was to be done is the subject of the next injunction.

3) *You shall not do any work.* They were to spend six days at work but refrain on the seventh, along with their whole household and even the animals. Thus it is stated rather negatively: they were told what **not** to do rather than what **to do**. The gap is filled and the positive supplied by two things:

- **Rest.** This is deduced from the fact that after creation "the Lord…rested on the seventh day." That it is good to have a rest day is not disputed, but that it is a command is not stated. Is not the pattern of work and rest a daily thing: the day to work and the night to rest? We today are blessed with artificial light and can work at any time of day or night. The people of Israel were not and the darkness forced them to cease working. The meaning of *rest*—(*sabbath*)—is *cessation*. God *ceased* (Gen. 2:2 NIVmg) from working, not because he was tired but because he had "finished his work" (Gen. 2:1). Obviously a day free from work is valuable for us personally and a national rest day is good, but it is not a law, and we don't need to campaign for such a law.

- **Worship.** This is probably derived from the fact that Israel's special worship days or festivals were called *Sabbaths* because work had to be laid aside to attend and celebrate them. But we must remember that these *Sabbath days* did not necessarily fall on the seventh day, in fact they could stretch over a whole week. Any day on which a ceremony was held was a Sabbath, because the people had to *rest* or *cease* from work in order to keep it. Also, we are told very little about the way worship was conducted on the Sabbath, if it was at all. From this point of view it does not seem to have been much different from what was done on the other days. The emphasis on worship increased as time went by, as we see from Psalm 92, which was especially composed "for the Sabbath day," and from Ezekiel 46:11 which gives instructions for worship in the temple on the Sabbath. The development of the synagogue system during the inter-testamental period also enhanced the use of the day for corporate worship. This is very evident in the time of Christ and the apostles. A day set aside to worship God is of great value, as we know from our churches, but it is not a law.

4) *The fourth commandment for Christians.* So what does the fourth commandment mean to us in these gospel days? Do we observe it as it stands, simply changing the day in honour of Christ's resurrection? Those who answer this question in the affirmative often appeal to the example of Christ, whose custom was to "keep the Sabbath" (e.g., Luke 4:14). But if we are to follow his example in the way we keep this Law, why do we not do so with all the other Laws? Why are we not circumcised on the eighth day and presented in the temple on the fortieth? The fact is that Jesus was "born under the law," not as our example, but as our Redeemer, "to redeem those under the law" (Gal. 4:4–5). Just as he took on sin in order to redeem us from it, so he did with the law.

But Jesus is not only Saviour; he is Lord—over everything, including the Sabbath. He claimed to be "greater than the Sabbath" (Mark 12:8). The occasion on which he spoke these words was when he permitted his disciples to pick some heads of grain to satisfy their hunger. When the Pharisees queried this, Jesus' reply was

The Sabbath was made for man, not man for the Sabbath. So the Son of Man is Lord even of the Sabbath (Mark 2:23–28).

He exercised his lordship on another occasion when he healed a man's shrivelled arm. His words further expand those of Mark 2:27:

Which is lawful on the Sabbath: to do good or to do evil, to save or to kill? (Mark 3:1–4)

So does that mean we can do as we "please on my holy day" (Isaiah 58:13)? In a sense, yes. If we truly love the Lord, his Word, his people and the means of his grace, it will *please* us to attend services for public worship and to use other parts of the day for reading, meditation and prayer, if we are blessed with having the day free, as many in our country are. But it is not a law that we go to church and spend our time reading the Bible and books about it rather than doing jobs or playing games. Why should Christians need a law to get them to church? Why should they have to be ordered to do what they most enjoy?

Robert Murray M'Cheyne is often held up as our example in this because of his famous words "I love the Lord's Day." Surely what he meant by this was not "I love the day as a day" but "I love what we do on that day:" meeting together for formal worship and ministry, plus informal fellowship and conversation, then retiring to spend time with family and friends, or even retiring from them to commune with God alone. It is sometimes said that the non-attendance of Christians at services is due to a low view of the fourth commandment, or that the reason why there is a smaller attendance at one of the services (usually the evening) is disobedience to the fourth commandment. But surely the reason is much deeper than that. If God's children do not want to meet with him and his people, to worship and hear his Word, to have fellowship together, it is because there is something lacking in their spiritual lives. Their relationship with God is weak, as is their love for their spiritual brothers and sisters. They have no conception of being members of a body, Christ's body. The principle is also relevant to the question of Christians working on Sunday. Some have to; others choose to. The problem is not that of working on the Lord's Day but of being absent from the worship and fellowship of God's people and the hearing of his Word.

When the writer of Hebrews alluded to this matter and encouraged Christians to assemble and not "give up meeting together as some are in the habit of doing" (Heb. 10:25), he gave as his reason, not the fourth commandment, but the ministry of "encouraging one another." Christians who will not meet on every possible occasion, unless prevented by circumstances beyond their control, show the barrenness of their hearts towards God and each other. They have no desire to encourage each other, probably because they are not being encouraged themselves. Spiritual encouragement is an infectious thing. Those who speak about it and enjoy it want to go and share it. If we need a law to do this it does not say much for the state of our souls. We are not governed by Sinai but by a soul in which Christ and his Spirit dwell. This approach is confirmed by the practice of Christ and the apostles, to which we now turn.

The Practice of Christ

At the time of Christ the Laws relating to the observance of the Sabbath were at their most highly developed stage. There were different schools of thought: the Essenes were the strictest, but the school of Shammai was quite strict, whereas the school of Hillel was more relaxed. Judgments from Jewish case law were recorded in the Halakah, later called the Mishnah. These gave details of what may or may not be done on the Sabbath, particularly regarding work. In principle what was prohibited was continuing to ply your normal trade on the Sabbath.

Jesus never set out to challenge these rules and he was careful to keep the Torah (the biblical law), but he did expose some of the hypocrisy of the Halakah. When Jesus healed on the Sabbath he was not breaking the Law, since he was not a doctor by trade. Nor were his disciples breaking it when they plucked and ate the ears of corn, since they were not farmers. He exposed the inconsistency of the Pharisees' practices when he charged them with refusing to heal a man on the Sabbath while being happy to rescue a sheep (Matt. 12:9–14).

He sought to bring them back to the principle that the Sabbath was to be a blessing not a burden: "the Sabbath was made for man not man for the Sabbath" (Mark 2:27). He appealed to Hosea 6:2 that God rates mercy above rituals and rules (Matt. 12:7). But he went further when he claimed "the Son of man is Lord of the Sabbath" (Mark 2:28). This not only made him equal with God but made him an interpreter of his Law. However, he never became explicit as to how he wanted the Sabbath to be observed in the new age. This must emerge in the course of time.

The Practice of the Apostles

We read in the New Testament of only one occasion on which Christians met together on the first day of the week: Acts 20:7–12. This was at Troas where Paul spent a week en route from Ephesus to Macedonia. The purpose was to 'break bread,' which no doubt means the Lord's Supper as it does in Acts 2:42. But this was accompanied by preaching from Paul who "kept on talking until midnight." This does not mean he had been speaking since first thing in the morning (!) for the first day of the week was not a holiday and the Christians would have assembled after work in the early or middle evening.

The only other reference to the first day of the week is 1 Corinthians 16:2 where Paul asks the Corinthian Christians to "set aside a sum of money" for him to collect later and take to the famine stricken Christians in Judea. There is no mention here of meeting for worship or ministry, which does not mean that they did not, simply that it is not explicit. So the evidence for Christians using the day as we do now is somewhat slender, but if this was the practice it could have been connected with Jesus' rising from the dead "on the first day of the week" (John 20:1) and appearing to his apostles later that day (John 20:19) and again a week later (John 20:26), although here there is no specific mention of this.

This may well have been the precedent for Sunday services and for calling it the *Lord's Day* (Rev. 1:10), but there is certainly no law given or even an apostolic injunction. Neither is there any indication that they regarded it as the Sabbath and transferred the Sinai legislation about the seventh day to the first day. In fact, as Jews, they appear to have continued to observe the Jewish Sabbath and the ministrations and observances of the temple and synagogue. For example, we find Peter and John "going up to the temple at the time of prayer" (Acts 3:1). As the apostles scattered and Gentiles came into the church, Jewish practices gradually loosened their hold on Christians. When the apostles and elders gathered in Jerusalem to discuss what should and what should not be imposed on Gentile believers (Acts 15), while there was discussion about circumcision as a requirement, there is no mention of the Sabbath. Yet the Sabbath was a covenant sign just as circumcision was. The latter was performed once for all on the eighth day of life, but keeping the Sabbath was done continually as a regular renewal of commitment to the covenant.

What we do find in the apostolic writings is their view of Sabbath days. Paul wrote to the Galatian Christians to warn them against trying to combine their new-found faith in Christ with Jewish legalism. His chief bone of contention is circumcision, but he also has something to say about the observance of days. In Galatians 4:10 he points out how they were "observing special days and months and seasons and years." This sounds as though the whole cycle of Jewish festivals was being imposed on them. It is true there is no reference to the Sabbath here. However, in Colossians 2:16–17 he made specific reference to the Sabbath, which he put alongside other special days and even the food laws, as observances from which Christians are now free.

> *Therefore do not let anyone judge you by what you eat or drink, or with regard to a religious festival, a New Moon celebration or a Sabbath day* (Col. 2:16).

The reason he gives is that these have been superseded by Christ:

> *These are a shadow of the things that were to come; the reality, however, is found in Christ* (Col. 2:17).

The institutions of the Law are a kind of silhouette—they point to a person but they are not that person. The prophets clarified this somewhat in their predictions of a Messiah, but Christ was still a shadowy figure until he came in person. Paul is saying that keeping special days is retreating from the substance back to the *shadow*, it is a retrograde step. The *shadow* (the seventh day Sabbath) has faded away not merely changed the day of its observance.

The letter to the Hebrews relates the Sabbath to the idea of *rest* (present and final) rather than to the fourth commandment. The Sabbath rest is not cessation from physical work but from "his own works," that is, striving for the final rest in heaven by the works of the Law:

...anyone who enters God's rest also rests from his own works, as God did from his (Heb. 4:10).

Christians are compared to Israelites on the verge of the Promised Land but who lost their opportunity through unbelief. This is why the writer uses Psalm 95:

I declared in my anger "They shall never enter my rest" (Heb. 4:3 quoting Psalm 95:11).

Hebrews is a letter calling Jewish Christians back from returning to the law and thus forsaking Christ; it relates the Sabbath to the idea of 'rest' (present and final) rather than to the fourth commandment. The Sabbath rest is not about a man resting from his daily work but from 'his own works,' that is, from striving for the final heavenly rest by 'the works of the law.'

To enter into the final rest in heaven it is necessary to enter the present rest by ceasing to strive for salvation by works and trusting in the work of Christ.

We have come to share in Christ if we hold firmly to the end the confidence we had at first (Hebrews 3:8).

Those who have Christ have no need to observe the Sabbath any more than they need to observe the Passover or Day of Atonement. We now have the true atonement, achieved by Christ on the cross. No Christian keeps the Day of Atonement. Similarly we have the true Sabbath rest which Christ has won for us through his atonement. We have peace *with* God and therefore the peace *of* God in our hearts. We no longer need the shadow for we have the substance. Of course, we still need rest and we need the opportunity to meet for worship and ministry, but we are no longer obliged to do these things on a particular day. This is all part of the burden of the Law which Christ has borne for us.

It has become clear from these passages that the coming of Jesus Christ fulfils the concept of rest tied up with the Old

Testament Sabbath and that because of the situation of the church between the resurrection and the *parousia* (return) of Christ, there is an "already" and a "not yet" to that fulfilment.[60]

We can therefore say that observing the Sabbath is part of a Jewish package which Christians, both Jew and Gentile, gradually cast off. Some were more reluctant than others to do this, but Paul was against railroading them into abandoning before they were ready those aspects of the Law to which they were clinging. He regarded them, not as wrong so much as weak and lacking in freedom. In Romans 14 he warned "the strong," who are enjoying the freedom of their faith, against judging such Christians adversely. This applies to those who still felt an obligation to the food Laws (Rom. 14:2–4) and to those who were observing special days (Rom. 14:6–8). Paul says such matters are between them and God, not for others to judge (Rom. 14:22).

The Post-Apostolic Church

The church of the second to fourth centuries only gradually became weaned from the Mosaic law. Many Jewish Christians continued to observe the Sabbath, but most Christians, especially Gentiles, took a more spiritual view of the day, regarding it as pointing to the heavenly rest, as in the letter to the Hebrews (Heb. 4:1–11). It has been fulfilled in Christ who has given us rest from striving to keep the Law for salvation and from a bad conscience which convicts us of failure to keep the Law and deprives us of the hope of heavenly rest.

> … outside Jewish Christianity, all second century references to the Sabbath commandment either endorse the metaphorical interpretation or reject the literal interpretation as Jewish, or both.[61]

---

[60] A.T. Lincoln, *From Sabbath to Lord's Day*, 214.

[61] R.J. Bauckham, "Sabbath and Sunday in the Post-Apostolic Church,"

Also, in the second century Sunday was becoming the recognised day for Christian worship. This was appropriate as being the day on which Christ rose from the dead. The purpose of the day was not rest (as in the Sabbath commandment) so much as public worship and the personal contemplation of Christ to aid the pursuit of holiness. The idea of rest in the commandment was fulfilled, not by having a special day of the week but spiritually day by day. There is no evidence that Christians desired a day of rest. This did not come about until AD 321 when on March 3rd the Emperor Constantine ordered Sunday as a day of rest. This may have been as much in honour of the sun as it was in honour of Christ's resurrection. Nor is there evidence that Christians were seeking a day free from work. The rest they sought was freedom from the burden of the flesh and the world. The contemplation of Christ risen, glorified, and preparing a place in heaven was a better way of achieving that than a day free from work. But whether work was done or not, Sunday became the Lord's Day during this period. However, seeing it as a Christian Sabbath on which the observance of the fourth commandment was transferred to the first day of the week and in which no work was done came much later in history, from about the seventh century.

The Mediaeval Church

Mediaeval thought was dominated by the teaching of Augustine (fourth to fifth centuries). He restored the Decalogue to a central place and thus exalted the Sabbath commandment. However, he saw the danger of *rest* becoming idleness leading to sensuality and said "It would be better they spent the day digging than dancing." So, like his forbearers he stressed that the rest is spiritual in the present time with the hope of a full final rest. It should be

From Sabbath to Lord's Day, 269.

used for contemplation, a kind of lay monasticism practised on one day of the week.

Christians in mediaeval times took this up and increasingly used Sunday for church services. Gradually Sunday work became condemned and eventually forbidden by law. In this way a 'Christian society' began to take shape. Another development was to draw a distinction between moral and ceremonial Law, which led to a more literal view of the Sabbath. Thomas Aquinas built on this with his teaching on Natural Law. This can be discovered by man's unaided reason apart from special divine revelation and is therefore justly binding on all men. The commandments of the Decalogue are natural law and therefore binding on all men. The Sabbath is a moral precept, celebrating both creation and the new creation and must be kept minutely. This became the standard Roman Catholic view, later enshrined in the Council of Trent (sixteenth century).

Sabbath and Lord's Day in Protestant Tradition

The Reformers broke with mediaeval Scholasticism and its teaching on the Sabbath and Lord's Day. Luther and Calvin taught the need for a time of bodily rest as a means of enjoying spiritual rest, but this was not a law so much as a type of Christ and his blessings. Since Christians cannot gather for worship every day, it was necessary for a day to be agreed upon, and the early church settled on Sunday.

The views of Luther and Calvin differed from each other somewhat. *Luther* took the view that a day for rest and worship should be observed weekly, but which day should be decided by the civil authority. *Calvin* was stronger than Luther on the law's permanent validity, but taught that obedience to it must come from the heart. As regards the Sabbath, the 'rest' is fulfilled by Christ and is therefore spiritual, as in Hebrews 4. The change of day from the seventh to the first was to avoid Judaizing and to commemorate Christ's resurrection. But it was to be used for mortification of sin and strictly observed. So while Calvin avoided Sabbatarianism, he opened the way to it.

Later continental theologians tended to revert to the mediaeval idea that natural law demanded a weekly day for rest and worship. The actual day chosen was not important, but simply a matter of order. In this way they sought to avoid legalism and to preserve Christian liberty.

In **England** the Sabbath of the fourth commandment was observed on Sunday with an emphasis on suppressing Sunday amusements. But the Puritans were not all in favour of inflicting punishments on Sabbath-breakers. Patrick Collinson records that

> when the official 'Homily of the place and time of prayer' threatened Sabbath-breakers with the dire penalty of the Hebrew who gathered sticks on that day, it was a Puritan who protested that this was to confound our Sunday with the Jewish Sabbath…which doctrine is superstitious.[62]

Richard Hooker, the foremost Anglican theologian of the time, developed the Scholastic teaching on the moral law which required Sunday to be a holy day, used for "Praise, bounty (works of charity) and rest." Expositions of the fourth commandment began to appear, notably by Nicholas Bounds in "The Doctrine of the Sabbath." He taught that the Sabbath has been binding on all since creation and the Decalogue made it part of the moral law. But the Westminster divines dissented from the view that the Decalogue was *"wholly* natural law" and called it "positive

---

[62] P. Collinson, "Essays on Protestant and Puritan," London 1983, p. 431. The quotation is taken from the Morrice MS B.1 p. 339 in Dr Williams' Library. It is quoted in Sinclair Ferguson: *Theonomy, a Reformed Critique*, p. 328.

law"—binding, not because it was 'natural,' like the law on the heart, but because it was the Word of God. The Decalogue came to be distinguished from the rest of the Mosaic legislation and its interpretation by Christ and the apostles. Since what was important was not the particular day but "one day in seven," the change from the seventh to the first day was justifiable.

The *rest* was to be used for worship, and the Directory of Public Worship gave advice on how to practise it. Some went into such detail that John Owen wrote that "a man can scarcely in six days read over all the duties to be observed on the seventh!" This declined in the eighteenth century but was revived in the nineteenth by Daniel Wilson, leading to the formation of the Lord's Day Observance Society in 1871. This body advocated that the state should regulate national behaviour, particularly what may be done on the Lord's Day, and emphasised the social value of a national day of rest. In spite of differences of detail, Sunday as an institution was never seriously questioned from the seventeenth to the nineteenth centuries.

Few **modern** Christians, apart from Seventh Day Baptists and Seventh Day Adventists, will be observing Saturday as a Christian festival to which they feel obligated by the fourth commandment. But many will think of Sunday as covered by the fourth commandment, with the day simply changed from day 7 to day 1 in honour of Christ and his resurrection. But, apart from the fact that there is no record of the apostles having spoken of changing the day, this is mixing the Law and the Gospel. *It is not Sunday that has replaced the Sabbath of the fourth commandment, but Christ and the gospel.* Seeing Sunday as a Christian Sabbath brings with it the danger of making Sunday a matter of conscience rather than grace. As already said, what matters is not the day but what we do on the day. It seems Sunday has been settled on as 'the Lord's

Day' when Christians meet in his honour, though this did not become official until after the time of the Roman Emperor Constantine.

The fact is that the idea of a Christian Sabbath free from work to enable services to be held in the morning is only possible where a nation is strongly enough influenced by Christianity to make laws that guarantee that freedom and at the same time get the citizens of that nation to use the day in this way. This is comparatively rare in the history of the nations of the world. It has been the case in the western world in those nations which formed what was called 'Christendom.' But it is far from the case in many other countries and in some periods of history for most countries. It was not the case for the early Christians either in Jewish territory or the Roman Empire. It is certainly not the case today for many nations of the world in which the gospel has gained a foothold. In Islamic countries Friday may be free but not Sunday. There Christians have to meet wherever they can, be it a Sunday or a weekday, be it 11 a.m. or 11 p.m., 6 p.m. or 6 a.m. This is increasingly happening in our own country where more and more go to work on Sunday. Are such disobeying the Law of God? Surely it is we who judge them who are out of step. Instead of judging we should organise ourselves in such a way that all have the opportunity to meet together.

Although not a commandment, a day free from work for everyone is a great blessing: to workers, to individuals and families of whatever faith or none at all, especially when it becomes a national institution. It has been proved to be good for health and even productivity. It is especially good for churches, enabling their members to come together for fellowship, worship and ministry.

If this is so, let us all agree to use these opportunities and means of grace to the fullest, for their own sake and in Christ's honour, not because of anything special about the actual day.

CHAPTER 10
THE LAW AND HOLINESS

What makes people *good*, or, to use the Bible word, *holy?* The descendants of Abraham through Jacob, the nation known as Israel, were set apart from others to be the people of God. *Set apart* is the meaning of *holy*. Because God was holy, they were to be holy too:

> I am the Lord your God; consecrate yourselves and be holy, because I am holy (Lev. 11:44).

But how exactly were they to do this? God gave them a covenant in the form of a code of laws which, if they kept fully, entitled them to be regarded by God as his "treasured possession...a kingdom of priests and a *holy* nation" (Ex. 19:5). This code of Laws was summed up in the Ten Commandments, as has already been seen. But the details are spelled out in the instructions God gave to Israel through Moses. Leviticus 18–19 is a clear and powerful example of this. Both chapters are based on the nature and character of God. Chapter 18 begins with the declaration "I am the Lord your God," which is repeated several times and forms the closing words of the chapter. Chapter 19 adds to this by beginning

> Be holy because I, the Lord your God, am holy (Lev. 19:2).

God is the Lord to whom they belong, and he is holy, so these two statements form the basis of his call to them to be holy, hence the word *because* in verse 2. The refrain "I am the Lord" is repeated continually throughout the chapter and again forms the closing words.

How successful was this method of promoting holiness? Some romanticise about Old Testament Israel as if the

people were models of virtue. Some even advocate the
imposition of the Old Testament Law, not just on the church,
but the nation too. Such people are probably judging by
those characters noted for their spirituality: Abraham,
Joseph, Moses, Samuel, David, some of the other kings and
the prophets, but these men were exceptions, and even they
were flawed, each one of them. While there was always a
faithful remnant, the generality of the people honoured the
Laws more in the breach than the observance. Nor did they
waste any time in doing this. In fact, even before Moses had
come down from Sinai, they were committing idolatry (Ex.
32:5), indulging in "revelry" (Ex. 32:6) and "running wild"
(Ex. 32:25). God called them "corrupt" (Ex. 32:7) and "stiff-
necked" (Ex. 32:9). They continued like this throughout their
history, which was why they had a succession of prophets
from Samuel to Malachi to call them back to loyalty to God.
The fact that Malachi was a prophet *after* the exile shows
that, while the exile had purged them of idolatry, it had not
made them more spiritually minded. In Acts 7 Stephen, the
first martyr, was able to look back over the entire history of
Israel, selecting key examples of their disobedience and
summing them up in words strongly reminiscent of those
words spoken by Moses at the beginning of their national
life:

> *You stiff-necked people, with uncircumcised hearts and ears! You*
> *always resist the Holy Spirit. Was there ever a prophet your fathers*
> *did not persecute? They even killed those who prophesied the coming*
> *of the Righteous One. And now you have betrayed and murdered*
> *him—you that have received the law that was put into effect through*
> *angels, but have not obeyed it* (Acts 7:51–53).

One of the great highlights of the Old Testament therefore
is the prophecy of Jeremiah 31:31–33 that God will

> *make a new covenant...not like the covenant made with their*
> *forefathers...because they broke it.*

It was to be a covenant in which the law was to be

put into their minds and written on their hearts.

It was called a law, not in the sense of being another rule of the kind which comprised the covenant of Sinai, but a law in the sense of a principle or word (as described in Chapter 1 of this book). The word *law* is used to sharpen the comparison between the covenants that Jeremiah is describing. This law is, of course, what we call the Gospel and it was to succeed where the old Law failed:

...through Christ Jesus the law of the Spirit of life has set me free from the law of sin and death. For what the law was powerless to do in that it was weakened by the sinful nature, God did by sending his own Son in the likeness of sinful man to be a sin offering. And so he condemned sin in sinful man, in order that the righteous requirements of the law might be fulfilled in us, who do not live according to the sinful nature, but according to the Spirit (Rom. 8:2–4).

These words were written by Paul after he had spoken of his own experience of failure under the Law (Rom. 7:7–25). Christians are far from perfect, but their behaviour in the world is of a far higher standard than that of Israel of old. Yes, there are warnings, rebukes and threats in the New Testament, but they are far outweighed by the commendations, encouragements and promises.

Another way to demonstrate this is to compare Christians with the unbelieving members of society. Who are the people who occupy the prisons, who commit the crimes, who appear before the courts, form the gangs, experience under-age pregnancy, make up the dysfunctional families, abuse their children, and so on? How many of these are Christians? Or look back over history, especially since the Reformation: Who founded the great and good institutions which are the strength of our society, such as hospitals, schools, industry, business and democratic government? All these are the work of Christians. Even the first scientists were Christians, as have been many of the great ones since them. Clearly there is something about the Gospel that changes human behaviour in a way that Laws do not, whether they are the laws of men (the law of the land), or even the Laws of God.

> Man's method of sanctification is by the Law, God's method of sanctification is by the Gospel; the former is by works, the latter is by faith.[63]

This does not mean we just jettison the Ten Commandments and the rest of the Sinai code as if it was useless. Paul said that "the law is holy, righteous and good" (Rom. 7:12) and that its failure was due not to any imperfection in it, but to the weakness of human sinful nature (Rom. 8:3). The law is, as was already said, the expression of the character of God, in the likeness of whom he made man. Fallen man needs something more and other than the law to make him holy. So the law does not have the same place for Christians as it did for the old covenant people of God. It is not the Christian's primary guide to a holy life. It is a secondary source and even then must be interpreted through New Testament eyes. This can be seen both in the individual (the Christian) and the community (the church), as we now proceed to see in a series of contrasts.

A. PERSONAL HOLINESS

Gospel holiness is superior to law holiness in a number of ways.

1. In its nature

---

[63] James Buchanan, *The Office and Work of the Holy Spirit* (Edinburgh: John Johnstone, 1844) 447.

Law holiness is *outward* and gospel holiness *inward*. In almost all instances the Law is about practical behaviour, the main exception being the tenth commandment, which, significantly, is the one which convicted Paul of sin and led him to Christ (Rom. 7:7–8). As a Pharisee Paul claimed that 'as regards legalistic righteousness' he was 'faultless' (Philip. 3:6). But when his spiritual life was searched he saw he was 'unspiritual, sold as a slave to sin' (Rom. 7:14). He needed an inward principle to make him truly holy. There were calls for 'circumcision of heart' under the old covenant (Deut. 10:16, Jer. 4:4), but there is little evidence that it often happened. Paul himself stated the principle in Romans 2:28–29 and taught that Christ alone could perform it (Col. 2:11). So the inward principle Paul needed was the work of the gospel, which transforms outward behaviour by first changing the inner nature. Not only does this enable a person to keep the commandments, but also to attain a higher standard than even the most meticulous observance of the commandments can achieve. Jesus prefaced his code of righteousness for his kingdom (the Sermon on the Mount) with the statement in Matthew 5:20:

> I tell you that unless your righteousness surpasses that of the Pharisees and teachers of the law you will certainly not enter the kingdom of heaven.

He proceeded to expand on this point in the rest of the sermon.

Some who hear about the kind of teaching contained in this book are afraid that if it catches on it will lower the standard of behaviour among Christians. They can relax. It will have the opposite effect. The standard required under the gospel, as exemplified in the Sermon on the Mount and the apostolic writings because it applies to inward attitude as well as outward behaviour, is infinitely higher than that of the Law and can only improve the holiness of Christians.

Indeed the best expositions of the Ten Commandments, such as those found in the Westminster Larger Catechism and Calvin's *Institutes*, all interpret the commandments in the light of the New Testament. I rest my case.

2. In its Character

The Law produces *legalistic* holiness and the Gospel *willing and free* holiness. Legalistic holiness consists in keeping Laws as duties which are obligatory rather than as standards which are desirable and beautiful and therefore chosen willingly. Legalists want everything regulated and therefore tend to add to the Laws given in the Scriptures. The Pharisees did this and Christ castigated them for it in Matthew 23. Gospel holiness looks on big broad principles, delights in them as eminently desirable, and therefore pursues them willingly and wholeheartedly.

Legalists also fail to distinguish between commandments and exhortations. They think that, because a statement is in the imperative mood, it has the force of an absolute moral law, and that to disobey it is sin. Many imperative statements in the New Testament, however, are exhortations or encouragements and therefore not laws. Laws are absolute and to break them is sin. Exhortations are like counsels—they advise us about the best way to proceed in a matter, and warn us against going other ways, ways which will lead to suffering. For example, Christ's "do not worry" (Matt. 5:25, 31) and Paul's "do not be anxious" (Philip. 4:6) are not commandments but encouragements which they back up with teaching about the faithfulness of God, who can be approached in prayer with these worries and anxieties. Preachers have been known to use these words to state bluntly that anxiety or worry is sin. For an anxious person to be told that is to make him even more anxious, not only about the original worry but about the fact that he is worried about it! This is not the gospel way, which comes to calm our fears and to encourage us to "cast all your anxiety on him because he cares for you" (1 Pet. 5:7), not to make us feel worse by convicting us for worrying. C.S. Lewis wrote:

> Some people feel guilty about their anxieties and regard them as a defect of faith. I don't agree at all. They are afflictions, not sins. Like all afflictions, they are, if we can so take them, our share in the Passion of Christ.[64]

Another example is Paul's exhortation not to be "yoked together with unbelievers" (2 Cor. 6:14). This is commonly taken to refer to marriage, although in the context it may have more to do with church fellowship. No doubt the principle can apply to marriage, but marriage to an unbeliever is not in and of itself a sin calling for church discipline. It is certainly an unwise thing for a believer to do and should be avoided if at all possible, that is, unless the alternative is worse. Our relationship with the people of the world is difficult enough without entangling ourselves in such a close relationship as marriage with them. This is not the same as calling it a sin in the way fornication and adultery are sins. Hence, the New Testament exhorts us to avoid it as unwise and harmful rather than forbids it as a sin.

An alternative way of expressing this is to distinguish between *commands* and *counsels*. Paul makes this distinction in his teaching on marriage in 1 Corinthians 7:25–36. In speaking against young women marrying "in the present crisis," he makes it clear that he has no specific "command of the Lord" but is giving his advice as an apostle.

Legalists also want to impose their man-made rules on others, which Christ accused the Pharisees of doing in

---

[64] C.S. Lewis, *Letters to Malcolm: Chiefly on Prayer*
   (http://www.goodreads.com/quotes/179501) accessed Feb. 6, 2014.

Matthew 23:4. Because *they* feel themselves to be obliged to keep their rules, they think everyone else should too. They tend to judge adversely those who do not follow their rules. Gospel holiness people are more understanding and tolerant. This applies particularly to matters which come under the heading of *worldliness*. When forms of entertainment began to proliferate a century or so ago, evangelicals began to compile an unwritten list of those which came into the category of worldly and frown on them. Christians who practised them were judged as worldly and disapproved of. This is very much like Pharisaic adding to the law.

Some legalists even go so far as to make God's gifts into laws. Couples in times gone by refused any form of contraception, including abstinence, because they believed that if God gave them a child they would be wrong to refuse it. What kind of God do they have? What kind of gospel do they believe? It still plays a part in Roman Catholic teaching against contraception and is not unknown in some Protestant circles today.

(a) In its Practice

The Law is concerned with *behaviour* and the gospel with *likeness to Christ*. Law holiness is by definition about knowing the rules and keeping them strictly. The majority of laws, both those in Scripture and those added to Scripture, are about external actions. While the New Testament has its moral demands and prohibitions, its main interest is in character. Jesus laid this down from the beginning when he went up a mountain, just as Moses had done long before, not to write a new rule book but to delineate the character of a member of his kingdom. These are the famous Beatitudes. They first describe Christ himself, who is the perfect example of them, and then those recreated in his image by the regenerating work of the Spirit.

Similar teaching is found in the ethical sections of Paul's letters. For example, in Galatians 5 he is putting the positive side to balance his anti-Judaistic teaching in the early part of the letter. In contrast to the life of the non-Christian (Gal. 5:19–20) he describes the character of one who bears "the fruit of the Spirit" (Gal. 5:22–23). How does he advise us to attain to this kind of life? His answer is not "keep the Law" (the Galatians were doing that!) but "live by the Spirit." Those who do this will be conforming to the Law far more than those who try to keep the rules but fail to exhibit love, joy, peace and so on. Jesus criticised the Pharisees on this score too:

> Woe to you, teachers of the law and Pharisees, you hypocrites! You give a tenth of your spices....But you have neglected the more important matters of the law—justice, mercy and faithfulness (Matt. 23:23).

It may be objected that no one kept the law more meticulously than Christ. He did this from the very beginning: circumcised on the eighth day, presented in the temple on the fortieth, becoming a *bar mitzvah* at thirteen, attending the synagogue on the Sabbath, sending the healed leper to the priest, and so on. This was because he was "born under the law" (Gal. 4:4) and lived under its yoke. But, why? "To redeem those who are under the law, so that we might receive the full rights of sons" (Gal. 4:4–5). He was not obliged to obey the Law, for no one was more entitled to "the rights of sons" than the Son of God himself! But he forewent those rights in order to keep the Law **for us**, to weave a robe of perfect righteousness to place on us in exchange for the filthy garments of our sin.

Yet though he kept the Law perfectly he still suffered the curse of a Law-breaker by being hung on a tree and enduring the abandonment of his heavenly Father. Why? To "redeem us from the curse of the law" (Gal. 3:13). By his life (his **active** obedience) he made a gift of perfect righteousness available to us, and by his death (his **passive** obedience) he removed from us the curse of death under the wrath of God. To those for whom he did this he gives the Holy Spirit to enable them to walk in his ways and become like him. In this way he fulfilled the original promise (Gen. 3:15) to reverse the curse of the fall and restore our original holiness, expressed in love and trust. In this way we share in Christ's holiness:

> *God disciplines us for our good, that we might share in his holiness* (Heb. 12:10).

5. In its Means

Law holiness is achieved by *human will and power*, gospel holiness by the mediation of Christ and the work of the Holy Spirit.

The question of *how* we become holy is central to the whole matter. Since Law holiness is external, that is, to do with good actions performed and wrong ones avoided, it is attainable through works done by man himself. It is quite within human power for a person to observe all the precepts of the Laws of Moses. There is a difficulty with the tenth commandment, but a strong will can even suppress the desire as well as the act of sin. So when the rich young ruler claimed, in answer to Jesus' spelling out the commandments: "All these I have kept since I was a boy" (Luke 18:21), Jesus did not contradict him; he simply added one the man had not considered: generosity to the poor, which exposed his selfishness and his covetousness. This is a kingdom or gospel requirement, and the man was unable to accede to it (Luke 18: 22–23).

Gospel holiness is unattainable by human effort, in fact man does not even have the will for it; he does not want it. The Jews are a good example of this, as Paul points out in Romans 9–10. The Jews had a good deal going for them:

> *Theirs is the adoption as sons; theirs the divine glory, the covenants, the receiving of the law, the temple worship and the promises. Theirs are the patriarchs, and from them is traced the human ancestry of Christ, who is God over all, forever praised!* (Rom. 9:4–5).

But where they failed was in their method of attaining to righteousness before God:

> *…the Gentiles, who did not pursue righteousness, have obtained it, a righteousness that is by faith; but Israel, who pursued a law of righteousness, has not attained it. Why not? Because they pursued it, not by faith, but as it were by works* (Rom. 9:30–32).

Earlier in his letter he had laid down this principle:

> *…no one will be declared righteous in his sight by observing the law; rather, through the law we become conscious of sin* (Rom. 3:20).

This was in fact Paul's route to the gospel way of holiness:

> *But now, a righteousness from God apart from the law, has been made known, to which the law and the prophets testify. This righteousness from God comes through faith in Jesus Christ to all who believe…Christ is the end of the law so that there may be righteousness for everyone who believes* (Rom. 3:21–22, 10:4).

It may be objected that in Romans Paul is speaking of justification, whereas holiness has more to do with sanctification. This is true, but sanctification is very much the fruit of justification. In Romans, after his clear teaching on justification before God through faith in Christ alone, he embarks on his teaching on sanctification in Romans 6. He bases this on justification in Christ. We not only believe he died for us in order to justify us, we believe we were "crucified with him" and therefore "died to sin" (Rom. 6:1–

4). Just as in his case resurrection to life followed his death, so for us:

> *If we died with Christ, we believe we shall also live with him* (Rom. 6:8).

In other words, there is a once-for-all holiness derived from Christ; as Hebrews 10:10 puts it

> *...by that will we have been made holy through the sacrifice of the body of Jesus Christ once for all.*

This is confirmed by Galatians 5:24 and Hebrews 10:14.

In those who believe this the Holy Spirit, the author of our faith and therefore instrumental in our justification, takes over. He is "the Spirit of holiness" (Rom. 1:4), the sanctifier, through whom we will not "gratify the desires of the sinful nature" (Gal. 5:16) but rather bring forth the fruit of holiness (Gal. 5:22–23). The gospel way of holiness is, then, not what we do by our determined effort ("works of the flesh"), but what Christ has done for us, and what the Holy Spirit does in us. In commenting on this passage about how the Spirit works in sanctification, John Owen wrote: "The Law drives them on and sin beats them back."[65] The Spirit succeeds where the law fails. Law is not strong enough to combat sin, but the Spirit succeeds where the law fails. "Let God give what he commands and command what he wills" (Augustine). So the way to avoid the sins of the flesh (Gal. 5:19–21) is not by going back to the law but by walking in the Spirit (Gal. 5:16).

6. In its Progress

Law holiness is *static*, Gospel holiness is *progressive*.

Law holiness is something you either have or you do not have. As James says, if you fail to keep just one Law, you are

---

[65] John Owen, *On the Mortification of Sin in Believers* (Wheaton, Ill: Crossway Books, 2006) 62.

just as guilty as if you fail in all of them (James 2:10–11). Law holiness is rather like those board games where, if you land on the wrong square, you have to go back to the beginning. This is why it is unattainable, since no one perfectly keeps the Law. This is because, as already seen, in law holiness we are on our own, we pursue it by "works of the flesh."

But with Gospel holiness we have two things which followers of Law holiness lack: the mediation of Christ, through whom our record is wiped clean, and the ministry of the Holy Spirit, through whom the living, reigning Christ dwells within us and bears his fruit. So we find the New Testament speaking about "growing in grace" (2 Pet. 3:18), the details of which Peter had spelt out earlier when he spoke of "adding to faith" (2 Pet. 1:5–7). This is not done by our own effort, but flows from "the divine power which has given us everything we need for life and godliness" (2 Pet. 1:3–4). Before speaking of what we add and how we grow he uses the phrase "for this reason" to show that God's power is the basis of our progressive sanctification. This continues through life, even through adversity, infirmity and old age, as Paul himself could testify:

> *Therefore we do not lose heart. Though outwardly we are wasting away, yet inwardly we are being renewed day by day* (2 Cor. 4:16).

7. In its Purpose

The purpose of Law holiness is to *escape punishment*, that of Gospel holiness to *see God*.

To imply that Law holiness is motivated by fear of punishment is not to deny the sincerity of those who claim they kept the law out of love for God (for example Psalm 119:47–48). Apart from the fact that these seem to have been in a minority in Israel, the law itself stresses the fear aspect: Leviticus 26:14–39 spells out the dire consequences of disobedience to the Law and violation of the covenant. There is enough there to frighten anyone into obedience!

The believer under the new covenant, however, has nothing to fear from the hand of God, for Christ has answered for his disobedience to the law. He enjoys appearing before God and cannot get enough of him. It is this that motivates his pursuit of holiness, for its outcome is the vision of God. Hebrews 12:14 says that "without holiness no one will see the Lord," implying that with holiness they will see the Lord. This is stated positively by Jesus in his Beatitudes:

Blessed are the pure in heart for they will see God (Matt. 5:8).

As already seen, God promised Israel that he "will dwell and walk among them" (Lev. 26:11–12), but this fell far short of the promise of Christ. The light of God's glory shone in the holy place, but was only seen by one man once a year—the high priest on the Day of Atonement. But the promise of Christ is for all believers every day.

8.   In its Rewards

Law holiness receives earthly, material and temporal blessings; Gospel holiness secures treasure in heaven.

In the preceding point, Leviticus 26:14–39 was quoted to show the curses of disobeying the law, which were to act as a deterrent to disobedience. It was preceded in Leviticus 26:1–13 by promises of blessings for obedience. These were such things as plentiful rain bringing fertility to the crops; peace through God's protection from their enemies and from wild beasts; and increase in population. In both curses and blessings God kept faith with Israel. In normal circumstances, they and their land prospered, but when they turned from him to idols and broke other laws, the rain was withheld, there was drought and famine, and eventually destruction and capture at the hands of their enemies, whom God used as instruments of punishment.

The gospel however, made no such promises. In fact, far from offering an easy, prosperous and successful life, it predicted that believers would suffer, not only the normal afflictions common to man, but persecution at the hands of non–believers. Such a man as Paul is an example of this. He suffered from a chronic affliction which even prayer would not remove (2 Cor. 12:7–9), though he does not tell us what it was. His journeys were by no means safe ones: he could be set on by robbers or wrecked at sea. He was treated unjustly by the Jews and even by Christians. However, he described all this as "light and momentary trouble" (2 Cor. 4:17) and said it was achieving an eternal glory that far outweighs them all.

This agrees with the teaching of Jesus who taught us not to worry about our earthly needs, and not to accumulate possessions, but rather by serving God to "store up treasures in heaven" (Matt. 6:19–24). He himself was the perfect example of this, for he lived with "no place to lay his head" and "endured much opposition from sinful men" (Heb. 12:3–4), even to the cross and its shame. Why? "For the joy that was set before him," the joy of being with the Father in heaven. It is this reward he offers us, though what it is in detail is not spelled out. It consists chiefly in the final fulfilment of the purpose of the gospel spoken of under the last point, that is, "seeing God." Our sight of him here is blurred by our own imperfections and the distractions of the world around us. When these are removed, "we shall see him as he is and be made like him" (1 Jn. 3:2).

There appear to be degrees of reward, as there are of punishment:

The servant who knows his master's will and does not get ready or does not do what his master wants will be beaten with many blows. But the one who does not know and does things deserving punishment will be beaten with few blows. From everyone who has been given much, much will be demanded; and from the one who has been entrusted with much, much more will be asked (Luke 12:47–48).

Those who endure persecution receive "a great reward" (Matt. 5:12). Rewards are allocated according to the quality of service and the degree of suffering endured. In the army every soldier who goes on a campaign receives a campaign medal, but those who perform great acts of bravery and suffer wounds and even death receive a special accolade. This is how it is with Christians: we all receive a reward for simply "enduring to the end," but those who perform great feats and undergo intense persecution receive special rewards. These rewards are bestowed in accordance with service for Christ:

the son of man is going to come in his Father's glory with his angels, and then he will reward each person according to what he has done (Matt. 16:27).

This means that our works are subject to testing at the day of judgment:

If any man builds on this foundation using gold, silver, costly stones, wood, hay or straw, his work will be shown for what it is, because the Day will bring it to light. It will be revealed by fire, and the fire will test the quality of each man's work. If what he has built survives, he will receive his reward. If it is burned up, he will suffer loss; he himself will be saved, but only as one escaping through the flames (1 Cor. 3:12–15).

As far as believers are concerned this appears to be the reason why believers as well as unbelievers come to God's judgment throne after death (Heb. 9:27). As regards condemnation the believer's judgment is over:

Whoever believes in him is not condemned (John 3:18).

I tell you the truth, whoever hears my word and believes him who sent me has eternal life and will not be condemned; he has crossed over from death to life (John 5:24).

As regards the allocation of rewards, believers come to have their works tested so that they may receive the appropriate reward. They

come before the judgment seat of Christ (to) receive what is due them for the things done in the body, whether good or bad (2 Cor. 5:10).

What this specifically is we are not told, but we will know when it happens. Those who trust in their obedience to the Law have no such promises.

Christ came not to abolish the Law but to fulfill it. If the Law's purpose is holiness, then it failed to achieve it. But where the Law failed the Gospel of Christ has succeeded. Those in him are made holy and go on to grow in holiness.

B.   CHURCH HOLINESS

When we come to the corporate aspect of holiness, holiness in the church, we find it is not so much a matter of *contrast* between law and gospel as *development and adaptation.* For the following examples I am indebted to Christopher Bennett's conference paper: "The Use of the Mosaic Law in the New Testament Church" in "The End of the Law" (Affinity Theological Study Conference, 2009).

1) 1 Corinthians 5: The Expulsion of the Immoral Man

Paul here tells the Corinthian church how they should deal with a case of serious immorality, one of exceptional seriousness involving the relationship between a man and his stepmother. Paul finds much help here in the Law but adapts it to the Gospel age.

- In 1 Corinthians 5:1 he describes the woman, not as the man's stepmother, but "his father's wife," recalling the

Law of Deuteronomy 22:30: "A man is not to marry *his father's wife;* he must not dishonour his father's bed."

- In 1 Corinthians 5:13, in instructing the church what to do about this he specifically quotes Deuteronomy: "expel the wicked man from among you." This is based on the sentence "you must purge the evil man from among you" which occurs several times in this part of the book of Deuteronomy: (Deut. 17:7, 19:19, 21:21, 22:21, 24, 24:7). But whereas under the Law this purging would have been done by execution, in the church it is done by excommunication.

- In 1 Corinthians 5:6–8 the idea of purging suggests another line of thought to Paul's mind—that of keeping yeast out of the Feast of Unleavened Bread. It requires only a little yeast to alter the whole nature of bread. Similarly it requires only one immoral person to contaminate a church. Therefore the immoral man must be put out, not just for the good of the church but for his own good "so that the sinful nature may be destroyed and his spirit saved on the day of the Lord" (1 Cor. 5:5). He develops this in an interesting way. The Feast of Unleavened Bread followed the Passover, at which a lamb was offered. But under the gospel this was discontinued because "Christ our Passover lamb has been sacrificed for us." This makes the purity of the church even more important, for without it we cannot "keep the festival," we cannot celebrate our salvation. Israel, after its first Passover, escaped from Egypt and celebrated on the far side of the Red Sea (Ex. 15), safe from its enemies. In Christ we celebrate our escape from sin, the devil and the wrath of God. But "the yeast of malice and wickedness" spoils this; therefore it must be "expelled," so that we can "eat the bread of sincerity and truth." The presence of an immoral person defiles the church's worship.

This example helps to show us the continuity and discontinuity of the old covenant. The people of God must always worship him in purity—"in sincerity and truth" and can therefore learn much from the Law. But this must be practised in a way which is in keeping with the gospel. So there is mercy for the offender: he is not killed but rather dealt with in a way designed to lead him to repentance. This is how "the Lamb of God who takes away the sin of the world" will be honoured.

2) 1 Corinthians 9:7–14: The Rights of Apostles

Paul is here affirming his right to receive financial support from the churches he planted and served. The context is the freedom of Christians from some Jewish customs that appeared to have the backing of the Law. The particular one under consideration is eating food that has been offered to idols, which would be an issue for Jews and Christians in a pagan city like Corinth. Theoretically, argues Paul, the Christian is free to eat such food, since an idol is not a real god anyway. However, in order not to damage the sensitive consciences of weak Christians, this right should be foregone. In a similar way Paul forwent his right to receive remuneration in order to maintain the principle that the gospel of salvation is free and cannot be purchased. In those days, when religious teachers or philosophers expected to be paid for their efforts, Paul refused remuneration lest he should be associated with these charlatans, and even more important, so that his gospel should be distinguished from their teaching. But for the sake of other preachers and succeeding generations he upholds the principle that preachers have a right to be supported by those to whom they minister.

The important point here is the way he argues for this—by using the Old Testament law and precedent. After giving examples of remuneration in common life in 1 Corinthians 9:7, he appeals to the Law: "Do not muzzle an ox when it is treading out the grain" (Deut. 25:4). In the age of the Law this would have been understood literally about the treatment of working animals. But Paul gives it a wider application. It applies not just to the animal who works, but the man, the farmer (1 Cor. 9:10). Widening it still further he applies it to the worker in God's harvest (1 Cor. 9:11). Christian preachers "sow spiritual seed" and therefore have a right to "a material harvest," that is, to remuneration.

As well as Law he also appeals to precedent (1 Cor. 9:13): priests and other temple workers are set aside from secular work to "work in the temple," and are dependent for their living on those whom they serve. They work for the benefit of the people as a whole and should therefore be remunerated for it: "those who preach the gospel should receive their living from the gospel" (1 Cor. 9:14).

So again we see the principle of continuity and discontinuity of the Law, and of its wider and deeper application to the gospel. Undoubtedly here Paul was guided by the Holy Spirit to give instruction to the church in all ages. Societies will not always be agricultural. Nevertheless, there are principles underlying God's will for godly people in all societies, including the industrial, which can show believers how to operate. He argues in a similar way in 1 Timothy 5:17–20. Such passages as these (and no doubt there are others) not only help us to use all Scripture in the life of our churches, but also to read the Old Testament with our eyes on the New Testament, and especially on Christ. The law's purpose was to produce not just holy individuals, but a holy people. The story of Israel is the story of the failure of that people to attain to holiness, for which they were so frequently punished and eventually rejected. But Christ has established a holy people—his church—and has thus fulfilled the Law. The apostles show us how to use the law in the light of Christ's redemption, and so to achieve this purpose.

CONCLUSION

I suppose there is one law from which none us will ever be free: that of Professor C. Northcote Parkinson, the famous 'Parkinson's Law,' which states that work expands according to the time available, or, to put it another way, there's always something waiting to be done, or even, as some would put it, 'there's no rest for the wicked!' This is certainly the case with writing books—they simply won't let you rest, they're always waiting to be continued, corrected, expanded and improved. Other things get neglected but eventually they have to be attended to.

This makes it sound as though writing this book has been a chore. This is far from the case, in fact the thought and study which underlie it and which have occupied about a quarter of a century of my life, has been one of my greatest blessings as a Christian and a preacher. Preachers and writers make wonderful discoveries in exploring the truth of God, which they feel they simply must share. This is what makes preachers and writers tick. So this has been no mere academic study to make our theology more correct and precise. It has great spiritual benefits.

First, it helps us avoid legalism. This was probably the greatest enemy Jesus had to fight in his ministry among the Jews. This is proved by the fact that it was the Pharisees who led the opposition against him, although of course the Sadducees hated him as well. Enmity against Jesus united these two contesting parties, not only because they were shocked at his claims and jealous of his popularity, but because he exposed their legalistic attitude. In this respect Jesus was unlike the prophets. Their calling was to denounce idolatry and immorality among God's people, hence their constant appeal to the Law. But this was largely purged away by the exile in Babylon, so that we do not find it in the preaching of the post-exilic prophets. Nor do we find it in the ministry of Jesus, but we do find him attacking legalism and hypocrisy, doing the right thing with a wrong motivation and a bad attitude.

Attitude is probably the best word to use in speaking of legalism. It has no distinctive theological errors; in fact it takes great pains to be correct in its doctrine as it does in the behaviour it advocates. But it breeds an attitude like that which Christ came up against in his ministry in the persons of the Pharisees and scribes. He did not denounce their doctrine or code of conduct, indeed he told his hearers to "obey them and do everything they tell you" (Matt. 23:3). But he added a warning not to follow their example, and gave specific instances of what he meant. This is always the danger which we face when we take great care over our doctrine and ethics. We are very precise to make these biblical, but inadvertently slip into an unbiblical attitude. There was a tendency in this direction after the Reformation, which cured us of Romanist idolatry and false doctrine, as well as setting a high moral standard, but later degenerated into legalism. Some of its marks are the following:

1) *A proud spirit which breeds censoriousness and judgmentalism.* This spirit is seen in the legalistic Jews in the time of our Lord. They judged Christ for "going to be the guest of a sinner" (Zacchaeus, Luke 19:7). They did not believe he could change people. This is why he told the parables about lostness in Luke 15:1–2. They said the same about his call of another tax-collector — Levi or Matthew (Matt. 9:11), which he answered in Matthew 9:12–13. Clearly they had not gotten this message by the time of the Zacchaeus incident.

This spirit is not confined to unbelievers, but is also found in believers. This is because the legalistic spirit fails to see that the reason we are different from other Christians is his grace not our goodness. Paul found this spirit in the Corinthian church:

> For who makes you different from anyone else? What do you have that you did not receive? And if you did receive it why do you boast as though you did not? (1 Cor. 4:7)

To hold to the doctrines of grace is not the same as having the grace of the doctrines. We can thank God for his grace to us but forget that that grace has so far been denied to others. But for the grace of God we would still be as they. 'Rethinking the Law' is a great antidote to this, but we can even forget this is a work of God's grace and become proud of our new understanding! This spirit can even come out in our bases of faith. Some of these stipulate doctrines which are not essential to salvation, such as the mode of baptism, the gifts of the Spirit, millenialist views and the present status of the Jews. To legislate on such points as this would mean that Christians who do not hold these views are unfit to be members of that particular church.

2) The legalistic spirit *breeds the tensions, divisions, quarrels and arguments* which are destroying unity both within and between our churches. Interestingly, Paul convicts the Christians in Galatia of this by an appeal to the Law which they prided themselves on keeping!

> The entire law is summed up in a single command: "Love your neighbour as yourself." If you keep on biting and devouring each other, watch out or you will be destroyed by each other (Gal. 5:14–15).

The *first prerequisite* of unity is not doctrinal correctness or moral perfection but humility. Humility and legalism do not go together.

3) This in turn *hinders our evangelism* because we judge the non-Christian instead of understanding him, that he is blind and graceless, as we once were. The Lord Jesus Christ expressed compassion to such:

> *When he saw the crowds he had compassion on them because they were harassed and helpless, like sheep without a shepherd* (Matt. 19:36).

On his final visit to Jerusalem, as he descended the Mount of Olives and saw the whole city spread out before him, "he wept over it" because they would reject and kill the one who could bring them true peace. But because this was "hidden from their eyes" they will experience utter destruction. He did not gloat over this; he wept. Legalists, however, tend to have the attitude that "it serves them right." We expect them to observe Christian standards without the Christian graces. Did *we*? Have we forgotten what we once were? Paul told Titus to remind the Christians of Crete that

> *At one time we too were foolish, disobedient, deceived and enslaved by all kinds of passions and pleasures.* [It was only when] *the kindness and love of God our Saviour appeared* [that this changed] (Titus 3:3–7).

Secondly, it sets us free from bondage and brings us into the freedom of the Spirit. In Romans 8:15 Paul says

> *You did not receive a spirit of bondage again to fear, but you received the Spirit of sonship.*

The law brought us into the bondage of fear, the fear of God's judgment. But since the gospel saves us from his judgment it also saves us from fear. Now we must avoid falling into bondage "again" by devising a new set of laws for Christians. There is a type of mind that wants everything regulated by laws and rules. "There should be a law against it!" is the cry that goes up when something happens of which we disapprove, especially if it harms us. This thinking can come into Christians regarding Christian behaviour and church practice. Concerning the above text, James Buchanan wrote:

> The word "again" implies that at some former time there did exist among God's people that spirit of bondage to fear which is here contrasted with the Spirit of adoption, and that they had even received it from God himself.[66]

The Spirit did not bring us out of bondage to the law of Moses in order to bring us back again to bondage to a Christian legalism. We are sons, not slaves and have a wonderful freedom to enjoy, as has been set out in Chapter 8.

Thirdly, it greatly broadens our whole idea of the Christian life. This is not, as many fear when they contemplate the possibility of becoming Christians, a life of simple and narrow rules about what we must and must not do. If that were so, the Bible would be only a few pages long! But the Christian life is rich and comprehensive. This is reflected in its vast literature. Anyone who sets out to describe it fully finds he has to produce a multi-volume work or preach to a congregation for many years, and even then not reach the end of it. The same applies to anyone attempting to live it. It grows and grows throughout the rest of their earthly lives; they are always making new discoveries; they find God's mercies are "new every morning." Unhappily this is not the case with all Christians; some, after a short while as Christians, never discover anything new; they try to live on what they first received, and they never move on to "fresh woods and pastures new." More often than not the reason will be their legal concept of the Christian life: that it consists of a few "do's and don'ts" which they try to observe. Of course there are "do's and don'ts" in the New Testament,

---

[66] James Buchanan, *The Office and Work of the Spirit*, Fifth Edition (Edinburgh, John Johnstone, 1844) 455.

but these are so swamped by the glories of the freedom of sonship that they are scarcely noticed! The free Christian is the sheep who is allowed to roam the fields and hills at will, not the one who is shut up in a pen or tethered to a post.

Fourthly, it gives an enhanced understanding of the structure of the Bible. It goes hand in hand with what is known as biblical theology, which traces the development of the theme of redemption from beginning to end, showing how the Old Testament and the Law were a preparation for the new covenant and the Gospel. *Rethinking the Law* is part of rethinking the structure of the Bible. But that is another story, although it is one that is being told by more and more authors in these days, to the great enrichment of our blessings. The more these things become known the more they will breed humility and understanding, unity and love, and a glorious sense of freedom.

> *Now the Lord is the Spirit, and where the Spirit of the Lord is there is freedom* (2 Cor. 3:17).

> *It is for freedom that Christ has set us free. Stand firm, then, and do not let yourselves be burdened again by a yoke of slavery...But if you are led by the Spirit, you are not under the law* (Gal. 5:1, 18).

APPENDIX ON MATTHEW 5:17–20

Christ came to establish "the kingdom of heaven" or "of God" (Matt. 3:2). He outlined its principles in the Sermon on the Mount (Matt. 5–7). In order to do so he "went up on the mountain" (Matt. 5:1, ESV), indicating he was going to do for "the kingdom of heaven" what Moses had done for the kingdom of Israel. Moses was God's chosen servant to establish the old covenant, and Christ was his servant to set up the new covenant.

In this great charter of the kingdom, Christ first of all set down the marks of character which the members of his kingdom bear in the Beatitudes (Matt. 5:3–16), in which the stress is on *attitudes* rather than *actions*. This immediately distinguished the new from the old, which is predominately about actions. After that, he set out examples of how members of his kingdom should behave, from Matthew 5:21 onwards. Putting character before behaviour shows one of the big differences between the old covenant and the new, in which there is both continuity and discontinuity. However, between these two sections in Matthew 5:17–20 he spoke of his own relationship to the old covenant, the law. This also shows continuity and discontinuity.

A. Matthew 5:17 BASIC PRINCIPLES

Negative: He did **not** come "to abolish the Law or the Prophets." It is important to notice that Jesus is not referring here just to the Mosaic law but to "the Law and the Prophets." This phrase, or more fully "the Law, the Prophets and the Writings" (Luke 24:44, which specifies the Psalms because it was the first book in the section known as the Writings) was the Hebrew way of describing what we call the Old Testament. In John 15:25 Jesus attributes quotations from Psalm 35:19 and Psalm 69:4 to the law. It is this, not just the Sinai Law, which Jesus said he had not "come to abolish." The word abolish is the same word as Jesus used in his prediction of the destruction of Jerusalem in Matthew 24, when he said its buildings will be "thrown down." Used in relation to the Scriptures it indicates a decisive rejection of their truth and significance, as if the Old Testament had nothing to say now that Jesus has come. If it does have something to say still, what is it? What is Jesus' relationship with the Old Testament?

Positive: What he came to do was to fulfill it, to carry out what the Old Testament was pointing to. This means more than bring out the full meaning, as he did when he compared the various Laws with his own teaching in Matthew 5:21 onwards. It refers to the message of the Old Testament as a whole. This implies that the entire book is prophetic, not just the words of the official prophets. The events, personalities and even the words and teachings of the Old Testament did not fully carry out God's original plan. They achieved much in setting up a kingdom of people special to God, but they did not fully achieve all he had planned, they did not fulfill it, they did not bring about its intended goal, as he did. They pointed to the one who will fulfill it, how he will do so and what he will achieve, that is, the salvation God planned in eternity. The law pointed to him, for the books of the law included some historical events as well as its ethical teaching and rituals. The events of Israel's *history* were typical, that is, a preview of his victory over sin and the devil; its *laws* pointed to the one who is perfectly holy; its *prophets* foretold him and its *writings* (Psalms, etc.) expressed a longing for him. So Jesus is not merely giving an explanatory preface to his teaching in the Sermon on the Mount, he is declaring what his kingdom is:

it is his reign—his life of perfect righteousness, the triumph of spirit over flesh, in which believers will share; his atoning work to cancel the huge debt which made us liable to God's judgment, and his resurrection from death to life, to end the reign of the great enemy of death - spiritual in the present, physical in the future and eternal thereafter. This is the kingdom which will fulfill what the old kingdom of Israel pointed to. The word *fulfill* is the word that sums up the New Testament, just as *promise* sums up the Old Testament.

This means that Jesus' teaching on the kingdom and its Laws is what the Old Testament was anticipating and which fulfills it. It is in this sense that Paul uses the word *end* in Romans 10:4: "Christ is the end of the law, so that there may be righteousness for everyone who believes." Christ's teaching fulfills the law and this is how believers in him and his teaching become righteous in a way they could not by obedience to Moses' Law. In Romans 3:31 Paul concludes his piece on justification by faith rather than Law by saying that faith "establishes the law." This carries the same meaning as *fulfill* in Matthew 5:17 and *end* in Romans 10:4. Faith in Christ is what the law pointed to.

B.   Matthew 5:18 AFFIRMATION

The word *for*, with which Matthew 5:18 (ESV) begins means that Jesus is confirming what he has just said: "I tell you the truth," literally "Amen, I say to you." *Amen* is a word of affirmation, 'the stamp of authority,'[67] usually put at the end of a statement or prayer.

To this he adds "until heaven and earth disappear," which shows that his return to heaven does not end the age of fulfillment, which goes on until his return to earth, when

---

[67] R.C.H. Lenski, *Interpretation of Matthew's Gospel* (Minneapolis, Minnesota, Augsburg Publishing House, 1943) 207-210.

all his foes become the footstool of his feet and his earthly kingdom gives way to the heavenly one (1 Cor. 15:24–28). In his earthly life he performed what was necessary to bring about his kingdom so that he could govern it from above.

This is developed in the words that follow about "the smallest letter and least stroke of a pen." The smallest letter in the Greek alphabet is the *iota* (corresponding to the Hebrew *yodh*) which was a little hook written underneath the word as a subscript, making it tiny. The least stroke was even smaller—the *keraia*, what we would call a slash, only smaller, which "distinguished a larger Hebrew letter from one which is similar."[68] This is a hyperbolical way of saying that what is written in the Old Testament must be carried out to the last detail. Here he abbreviates the title of the Old Testament to just "the Law." Everything in it must be accomplished, that is, all that it was pointing to must *happen, take place,* or *be carried out,* which is the meaning of the word *accomplish.* Much was carried out during his earthly ministry, and much more between that and his return. It is being carried out at this moment and will go on being carried out until the end of the world.

C. Matthew 5:19 OUR OBLIGATION

Jesus has been speaking of his own ministry as foretold in the Old Testament and carried out by him in his life here. But the kingdom is more than the King; it includes the King's subjects, those in the kingdom, his believing disciples. They have their obligations to him, their King, the one who is the chief subject of the Old Testament and has carried out its promises. What are these obligations? They are to keep its commandments, and teach others to do so too. This is expressed in a negative way here: breaking them

---

[68] Ibid.

and teaching others to break them, but the best way to avoid breaking them is to keep them!

What are these commandments? They are the commandments of the kingdom issued by the King. Here Jesus takes the term used of Old Testament Laws (*entole*, meaning commandments) and uses it of his own commands. Nor is this the only place he does so. The word is used in John 13:34 of his new commandment to love as he loved, and in John 14:15 it is used of the obligation of obedience imposed by their professed love for him. This is also true of John 14:21, and in John 15:10 it is used of their obedience to his commands as the way to remain in his love; in John 15:12 the command to love each other is repeated. It is also used in 1 John 3:22 of his command to believe, as it is again in 1 John 5:2–3: to believe in his name and love each other.

The verbal form (to command) is used in John 14:31 and again in John 15:14. Matthew 28:20 is an interesting use of this verbal form, for not only does he command his disciples to go into the world and make disciples of the nations, but also to "teach them to obey everything I have commanded you." This corresponds to Matthew 5:19 which obliges his disciples not only to obey his commands themselves but to teach others to do so as well. Believers are to keep his command to preach him in the world and call upon those who hear to keep his commands, believe on him and love one another.

The commands are not all of equal importance; there are lesser ones and greater ones. For example, Jesus said that love for God and our neighbour is the greatest of them all (Matt. 22:34–40). On the other hand he spoke of being faithful in the lesser things as the way to learn faithfulness in the greater (Luke 16:10).

He speaks also of the rewards of obedience. Those who fail to obey are least in the kingdom. They are **in** the kingdom, for this is not about moral disobedience or sin, which is punished with hell fire. It is about discipleship and corresponds to his teaching on rewards in Luke 19:11–27 (the parable of the minas) and to Matthew 25:14–30 (the parable of the talents). This idea is also taught by Paul in 1 Corinthians 3:10–15. There are degrees of reward as there are of punishment (Luke 12:47–48).

Correspondingly, those who "practise and teach these commands will be called great in the kingdom of heaven." They are more highly regarded both by himself and others in the kingdom. This is not therefore about the moral law laid on all men, but about Christ's teaching and commands in the gospel. Lest we should think this means that the greatest in the kingdom are its teachers because of their knowledge and office, on another occasion he specified that a little child who believes in him is "greatest in the kingdom" (Matt. 18:1–4). Indeed we all have to become like little children to enter the kingdom; we must not trust in whatever knowledge, office or standard of behaviour we have attained, but become as nothing.

This leads us naturally to verse 20 which is also about entering the kingdom.

D. Matthew 5:20 A WARNING AGAINST FAILURE TO KEEP THE OBLIGATIONS

Here he goes further than in Matthew 5:19: obedience to the commandments of the kingdom, which are the commandments of Jesus the King, is not just about our position in the kingdom, but whether we have entered it at all.

To clarify this he does not give a list of commandments, sins or virtues, but takes the Pharisees and teachers of the

Law as examples. These people taught the Laws of Moses, the Sinai code, and enlarged on it with detailed rules which to them were necessary to keeping the original Laws. Moreover, they themselves practised their laws and rules meticulously. But they were on completely the wrong lines. There was no way into the kingdom of heaven by works of the law or office-bearing, and therefore no way to attaining greatness in the kingdom by going down that road. When he castigated the Pharisees in Matthew 23, he told them they were scrupulous about the details of the law but "neglected the more important matters—justice, mercy and faithfulness" (Matt. 23:23). Though these were not entirely absent from the Law of Moses, they were not given the priority that Jesus gave them. Those who neglected them showed they were not just least in the kingdom, they were outside it altogether.

In his encounter with the Pharisee Nicodemus in John 3 Jesus issued the basic command about entrance into the kingdom: "you must be born again" (John 3:7). There is no way of keeping his other commands (to believe in him, love him and his people and evangelize the world) without this initial change of nature. This was why he set up a child as the greatest: the child brings no baggage, he comes with nothing.

That Christ's laws are higher than Moses' law was acknowledged by the Puritans:

> Far from there being any reduction in the obligation resting on the believer, the facts are opposite, for "as Christ came to raise the comfort of the creature to the highest, so also the duty of the creature to the highest," and "in the Christian religion all moral duties are advanced and heightened to the greatest perfection."[69]

---

[69] Kevan, *The Grace of Law*, quoting Thomas Manton on Ephesians and

All this is made possible by what he said in Matthew 5:17 about his having fulfilled what the Old Testament Scriptures were pointing to. It is that fulfillment that enables us to have a place in the kingdom, to keep the commandments of the kingdom, and have a righteousness acceptable to God. It is all due to the fact that he fulfilled the great offices of Old Testament times: he became the PROPHET whose teaching is God's final word (Heb. 1:1), the PRIEST who has offered himself for sinners as the lamb of God, the all-sufficient sacrifice offered once for all, and the KING compared with whom the best of Israel's kings were only pale shadows. Even David, the one most like him, sinned grievously and needed salvation himself. This is the one who has brought in the kingdom of heaven as opposed to any kingdom of the earth, the kingdom of God rather than the kingdom of man, and who alone has the authority to admit sinners into it.

There is a good summary of the various view of this passage held by theologians down the ages in *New Covenant Theology*.[70]

James, 176.

[70] Tom Wells and Fred Zaspel, *New Covenant Theology* (Frederick, MD, New Covenant Media, 2002) 79-90.

Scripture Index

Genesis
1:28, pp. 13, 18
1:28–30, p. 17
2, pp. 153, 158
2:1, p. 160
2:1–3, p. 152
2:2, pp. 153, 160
2:2–3, pp. 149, 158
2:3, pp. 152, 154, 155
2:15, pp. 13, 17
2:16, p. 18
2:17, pp. 10, 12, 18
2:17 f, p. 12
2:19–20, p. 17
3:6, p. 53
3:15, pp. 80, 86, 102, 116, 183
4:1, p. 52
4:2–8, p. 19
4:6–7, p. 21
4:8, p. 52
4:9, p. 53
4:19, pp. 22, 52
4:23, pp. 22, 52
5, p. 23
6:4, p. 22
6:9–13, p. 52
6:11, p. 22
9:5–6, p. 22
9:6, p. 52
9:22, pp. 22, 51
12:1–3, pp. 48, 71, 107
12:3, p. 115
12:10–20, p. 22

12:11–13, 20:2, p. 53
14:18–20, p. 48
15:6, pp. 1, 33, 80, 134
16:1–4, p. 22
17:1, p. 127
17:1–8, p. 33
17:8, p. 72
17:14, p. 36
18:10–15, p. 49
19:4–5, pp. 22, 53
19:9, p. 72
19:30–35, p. 52
19:30–38, pp. 22, 52
20:1–7, p. 22
20:6, p. 22
20:11, p. 21
26:5, p. 23
26:7, p. 53
26:9–11, p. 22
27, pp. 22, 53
27:19, p. 52
31:5, p. 53
31:9, p. 48
31:19, pp. 22, 53
31:34–35, pp. 22, 53
34, p. 53
34:13–17, p. 53
34:25–26, p. 52
35:22, p. 52
37:31–32, p. 53
38:15, p. 53
49:4, p. 52

Exodus

2:11–12, p. 52
3:18, 4:23, 5:1, 3, p. 23
4:24–26, pp. 36, 73
5:21, p. 50
9:27–28, p. 50
10:10, p. 50
12–13, p. 23
13:9, p. 23
14:10, p. 50
15, p. 192
15:1–18, p. 23
16, pp. 51, 155, 159
16:2–3, p. 50
16:5, p. 155
16:22–25, p. 23
16:23, pp. 51, 155
16:23, 30, p. 149
16:24, p. 155
16:26, p. 155
16:27, pp. 23, 155
16:28, p. 24
16:28–29, p. 155
17:7, p. 50
19:5, pp. 35, 108, 156, 158, 175
19:5–6, pp. 33, 35, 72
19:6, p. 91
19:8, pp. 6, 38, 72, 108
19:12–13, p. 39
19:14, p. 39
19:15, p. 39
19:16, p. 39
19:17–19, p. 39
19:20, p. 39
19:22, 24, p. 40
20, pp. 59, 153, 155
20: 8–11, p. 149

20:1, p. 35
20:2, 12, p. 54
20:3, p. 48
20:4–6, p. 48
20:7, p. 49
20:8–11, p. 51
20:11, pp. 155, 158
20:12, pp. 36, 51, 157
20:13, p. 52
20:14, p. 52
20:15, p. 53
20:16, p. 53
20:17, p. 53
20:22, p. 30
20:22–23:19, p. 30
20:22–26, 23:14–19, p. 30
20–40, p. 27
21:1, p. 54
21:1–11, p. 61
21–22, p. 30
22:1–15, p. 60
22:20, p. 56
22:28, p. 59
23:10–31:17, p. 56
23:14–19, p. 56
23:23–33, p. 56
24, pp. 56, 108
24:3–8, pp. 36, 156
24:8, p. 73
25–31, pp. 30, 56
31:13, 16, p. 156
31:13–17, p. 36
31:15–16, p. 73
31:16, p. 24
31:16–17, p. 73
32, pp. 49, 56
32:5, p. 176

32:6, p. 176
32:7, p. 176
32:9, p. 176
32:15–16, p. 54
32:25, p. 176
33, p. 56
34, p. 56
34:28, pp. 35, 47, 156
35:1–5, p. 56

Leviticus
1–18, p. 56
4–8, 26, 28–31, p. 57
7:37, p. 6
11:44, p. 175
11:44–45, p. 42
11:44–45, 19:2, p. 95
12–15, p. 42
18, p. 60
18:5, p. 126
18–19, p. 175
19, pp. 30, 56, 96
19:2, p. 175
19:3, p. 59
19:5, p. 30
19:9–10, pp. 42, 61
19:12, p. 59
19:13, p. 96
19:13–18, p. 61
19:14, pp. 42, 96
19:18, pp. 55, 61
19:32, p. 42
19:33, p. 43
20, p. 57
21–27, p. 57
23, p. 30
25:2, p. 157

25:8–12, 28, p. 157
26:1–13, p. 188
26:11–12, p. 187
26:14–39, pp. 187, 188
26:15, pp. 36, 156

Numbers
3–10, p. 57
9:1–14, p. 42
15:38–40, p. 83
28, p. 30

Deuteronomy
4:1, p. 126
4:2, p. 37
4:5–8, pp. 37, 117
4:6, 8, p. 95
4:13, pp. 35, 47, 72
4:32–40, p. 40
4:44, p. 6
4:45, p. 6
5, pp. 57, 153
5:2, pp. 72, 156
5:2–3, p. 35
5:15, p. 158
5:32–33, p. 73
6:1, p. 28
6:1–9, p. 57
6:4, p. 57
6:4–5, p. 55
6:13, p. 57
7–13, p. 57
8:1, p. 126
8:5, 32:7–15, p. 129
10:4, p. 47
10:12–13, pp. 9, 57
10:16, pp. 58, 179

10:18, p. 96
10:19, p. 96
11, p. 58
14–18, p. 57
17:7, 19:19, 21:21, 22:21, 24,
24:7, p. 191
17:18–20, p. 37
18:15–20, p. 106
19, p. 61
19:15–21, p. 60
19:15–22, p. 60
19–21, p. 60
20, p. 60
21, p. 60
21:12–36, p. 60
21:18–21, p. 60
21:22, p. 60
21:23, p. 85
22:1–4, pp. 60, 96
22:8, p. 31
22:13–30, p. 60
22:30, p. 191
24:1–4, p. 60
24:5, p. 96
24:6, 12–13, p. 96
24:14–15, 19–21, p. 96
25:4, p. 193
26:16–30:20, p. 108
27:1–8, p. 58
27:9–28:68, p. 58
27:26, p. 79
27–28, pp. 36, 73
28, pp. 85, 128
29, p. 58
29:1, p. 73
29:18, p. 58
31:15, p. 58

31:16, p. 58
31:16, 20, p. 36
31:16, 20–21, p. 73
31:24–26, p. 36
32–33, p. 58

Joshua
24:2, pp. 22, 48, 107
24:19–20, p. 40

Judges
2:13–14, p. 76

2 Samuel
6:7, p. 76

1 Kings
2:3, p. 6

2 Kings
17:34–41, p. 74

2 Chronicles
12:1–2, p. 74
36:21, p. 156

Ezra
10, p. 117

Nehemiah
10:31, p. 36
13:6, p. 101

Job
1:1, p. 23
1:5, p. 50
2:10, p. 51

3:1–5, p. 51
29, p. 23
38:7, p. 17

Psalms
14:2–3, p. 44
18:16–17, p. 74
19:7, p. 83
35:19, p. 202
50:15–16, p. 124
51, p. 81
51:6, p. 122
69:4, p. 202
78:10, p. 74
82:6, p. 5
92, p. 160
95, pp. 153, 166
95:11, p. 166
103, p. 92
110, p. 81
119, pp. 7, 43, 123
119:47–48, p. 187
119:97, p. 44
148, p. 17

Proverbs
1:8, p. 7

Isaiah
1:4–7, p. 76
1:10, p. 7
2:2–4, p. 101
5:20, p. 124
7:14, p. 105
11, p. 81
42:4, p. 7
51:4, p. 7

53, pp. 81, 104
53:9, p. 119
58:13, p. 161
58:13–14, p. 157
61:1, p. 131

Jeremiah
4:4, p. 179
11:1–8, p. 74
31:31–33, p. 176
31:31–34, pp. 109, 116
31:33, pp. 10, 89, 122, 140
31:34, p. 116

Ezekiel
20, p. 74
20:7–8, p. 48
20:12–13, p. 157
20:12–20, pp. 24, 36
36:25–26, p. 140
36:27, p. 140
44:7, pp. 36, 73
46:11, p. 160

Hosea
6:2, p. 164
11:1, p. 129

Micah
6:8, p. 9

Malachi
2:10, p. 36
2:10–12, p. 73
3:1, p. 33
4:2, p. 102

Matthew

1:21, p. 105

2:15, 18, 23, 4:15–16, 8:17, p. 105

3:2, p. 201

3:15, pp. 84, 118, 139

5, pp. 24, 84, 106

5:1, p. 201

5:3–16, p. 201

5:8, p. 187

5:12, p. 189

5:16, p. 91

5:17, pp. 5, 61, 84, 109, 110, 139, 201, 203, 207

5:17–18, pp. 45, 100, 105, 111

5:17–20, pp. 99, 100, 105, 106, 111, 201

5:17–48, p. 106

5:18, pp. 5, 84, 100, 203

5:19, pp. 100, 105, 111, 204, 205, 206

5:19–20, p. 100

5:19–21, p. 106

5:20, pp. 1, 5, 100, 107, 111, 179, 206

5:21, pp. 201, 202

5:21–26, p. 65

5:21–42, p. 111

5:25, 31, p. 180

5:27–30, p. 65

5:31–32, p. 65

5:33–37, p. 66

5:38–39, p. 110

5:38–41, p. 65

5:43–48, pp. 24, 111

5–7, p. 201

6:1, p. 106

6:1–18, p. 112

6:19–24, p. 189

6:25–34, p. 112

6:33, p. 107

6–7, pp. 106, 112

7:1–5, p. 112

7:6, 15–23, p. 112

7:24–27, p. 112

9:11, p. 196

9:12–13, p. 196

9:13, p. 97

11:11–13, p. 100

11:13, pp. 6, 109

12:6, p. 104

12:7, p. 164

12:9–14, p. 163

12:31–32, p. 63

12:33–37, p. 63

15:1–20, p. 104

16:27, p. 189

18:1–4, p. 206

18:16, p. 31

19, p. 60

19:1–12, p. 65

19:4–6, p. 115

19:16–22, p. 88

19:16–30, p. 127

19:36, p. 198

21:42, 22:41–45, 26:54, p. 105

22:15–22, p. 64

22:34–40, pp. 14, 24, 205

22:35–40, p. 112

23, pp. 180, 207

23:3, p. 196

23:4, p. 181

23:23, pp. 183, 207

24, pp. 104, 202

25:14–30, p. 206
27:46, p. 85
28:1, p. 149
28:20, p. 205

Mark
1:14, p. 100
1:44, p. 104
2:21–22, p. 99
2:23–3:6, p. 158
2:23–28, p. 161
2:27, pp. 158, 161, 164
2:28, p. 164
3:1–4, p. 161
7:14–22, p. 143
7:20–23, p. 67
12:8, p. 161
12:28, p. 55
12:29, pp. 57, 62
12:29–31, p. 67
12:40, p. 66
12:44–49, p. 66
16:2, p. 149

Luke
1:46–47, p. 92
2:10–11, p. 113
2:21, p. 82
2:22–24, p. 82
2:39, pp. 82, 118
2:41–42, p. 82
2:51, pp. 64, 82
4:14, p. 161
4:16, p. 82
4:16–21, p. 105
4:18, p. 131
5:14, 17:14, p. 83

6:31, p. 31
8:40, p. 83
10:26, 18:20, p. 83
11:1–13, p. 62
11:11–13, p. 92
11:46, p. 83
12:13–15, p. 67
12:47–48, pp. 189, 206
13:10–17, 14:1–6, p. 83
15:1–2, p. 196
15:11–32, p. 62
16:10, p. 205
16:16, pp. 109, 114
16:17, p. 114
16:18, p. 114
18: 22–23, p. 184
18:21, p. 184
19:7, p. 196
19:11–27, p. 206
22:19, p. 159
22:20, p. 109
24:1, p. 149
24:27, pp. 81, 100
24:44, pp. 5, 81, 100, 114, 201
24:45, p. 123

John
1:17, pp. 6, 108, 115
1:29, p. 119
2:19–21, p. 104
3, p. 207
3:3, p. 106
3:3, 5, p. 140
3:7, p. 207
3:18, p. 190
4, p. 92
4:23–24, pp. 142, 143

4:24, p. 92
5:16–17, p. 154
5:17, p. 152
5:19, 9:16, p. 83
5:24, p. 190
5:30, p. 81
5:45, p. 83
5:46, p. 108
8:17, p. 83
8:20, p. 118
8:29, p. 81
8:31–36, p. 131
8:36, p. 131
10:18, p. 81
10:34, p. 5
10:34–35, p. 99
12:49–50, p. 81
13:34, pp. 146, 205
13:34–35, p. 111
14:15, p. 205
14:21, p. 205
14:31, p. 205
14–17, p. 106
15:10, pp. 81, 205
15:12, p. 205
15:14, p. 205
15:25, p. 202
16:8, p. 88
20:1, pp. 149, 164
20:19, pp. 149, 164
20:26, pp. 149, 165

Acts
2:42, p. 164
3:1, p. 165
4:19–20, p. 65
4:19–20, 5:29, p. 148

7, p. 176
7:51–53, pp. 102, 176
10, p. 144
13:39, p. 128
15, pp. 117, 165
15:28–29, p. 117
20:7–12, pp. 149, 164
28:23, p. 87

Romans
1:1, p. 130
1:4, p. 185
1:5, p. 116
1:17, p. 126
1:18, p. 79
1:20, p. 79
1:22, 25, p. 48
1:29, p. 67
1:32, p. 13
1–11, p. 44
2, p. 79
2:2–3, p. 89
2:12–15, p. 6
2:14, pp. 6, 131
2:14–15, pp. 9, 98
2:15, pp. 13, 47
2:28–29, p. 179
3, pp. 125, 133
3:2, p. 115
3:8, p. 25
3:10, p. 79
3:19, pp. 5, 6, 131
3:19, 21, p. 8
3:19–20, pp. 79, 133
3:20, pp. 70, 97, 124, 185
3:20, 7:7, 13, p. 89
3:20–23, p. 125

3:21–22, 10:4, pp. 134, 185

3:25, pp. 4, 119, 126

3:26, p. 3

3:27, p. 3

3:28, p. 125

3:31, pp. 109, 125, 203

4:1–5, p. 4

4:4–24, p. 33

4:23–24, p. 1

5:1–2, p. 129

5:5, p. 112

5:6–8, p. 138

5:12, p. 70

5:12–14, p. 20

5:13, pp. 8, 17, 25

5:13–14, pp. 17, 47

5:15, 17, 18, p. 75

5:16, p. 128

5:20, pp. 69, 70, 75

6, pp. 131, 185

6:1, p. 136

6:1–4, p. 185

6:8, p. 185

6:14, p. 131

6:15–18, p. 13

6:23, p. 17

7, pp. 11, 19, 96, 132

7:1–6, p. 132

7:2, p. 71

7:4, p. 132

7:5, p. 71

7:7, p. 70

7:7–8, p. 178

7:7–11, p. 134

7:7–25, p. 177

7:8, 11, 13, p. 70

7:8–11, p. 89

7:8–24, p. 88

7:9–11, p. 134

7:10, p. 127

7:10–13, p. 1

7:12, pp. 37, 124, 178

7:13, p. 70

7:14, pp. 71, 122, 179

7:15–16, p. 71

7:15–23, 25, p. 71

7:17, p. 71

7:21, pp. 4, 122

7:22, p. 38

7:23, p. 4

7:24, pp. 71, 89

7:25, p. 71

8:1, p. 128

8:1–4, p. 141

8:1–4, 10:4, p. 116

8:2, pp. 135, 139

8:2–4, pp. 4, 177

8:3, pp. 84, 178

8:3–4, pp. 1, 67, 84, 124, 126, 135, 139

8:14, p. 130

8:15, p. 198

9:4–5, pp. 116, 184

9:5, pp. 91, 116

9:30–32, p. 185

9–10, p. 184

10:1–7, p. 130

10:3, p. 133

10:4, pp. 45, 84, 108, 109, 203

10:5, p. 127

10:8–13, p. 130

12:2, pp. 11, 44

12:19–21, p. 65

13, p. 147

13:1–7, pp. 64, 93
13:2, p. 65
13:8–10, p. 67
13:10, p. 24
14, p. 167
14:1, p. 146
14:2–4, p. 167
14:5–8, p. 63
14:6–8, p. 168
14:15, p. 146
14:22, p. 168

1 Corinthians
2:12, p. 123
3:10–15, p. 206
3:12–15, p. 190
4:7, p. 197
5, pp. 34, 191
5:1, p. 191
5:5, p. 191
5:6–8, p. 191
5:13, p. 191
6, p. 34
6:12, pp. 144, 145
6:15–20, p. 35
7, p. 65
7:12–13, p. 117
7:25–36, p. 181
8:9, p. 145
9, p. 147
9:5–6, p. 147
9:7, p. 193
9:7–14, p. 192
9:9–10, p. 94
9:10, p. 193
9:11, p. 193
9:11, 15, p. 147

9:13, p. 193
9:14, p. 193
9:19–21, p. 94
9:21, pp. 13, 133, 141
10:23, p. 144
10:23–24, p. 146
10:32, p. 146
11:20, p. 151
13, p. 92
14:15, p. 92
14:16, p. 91
15:24–28, p. 203
15:56, pp. 8, 71
16:2, p. 164

2 Corinthians
3, p. 122
3:3, pp. 122, 141
3:6, p. 31
3:7–18, p. 122
3:17, p. 200
4:16, p. 187
4:17, p. 188
5:10, p. 190
5:21, p. 138
6:14, p. 181
6:14–7:1, p. 145
7:1, pp. 25, 140
8–9, p. 66
12:7–9, p. 188

Galatians
2, p. 132
2:11–21, p. 144
2:16, p. 124
2:19, p. 132
3:6–9, p. 1

3:10, pp. 79, 127
3:10–19, p. 33
3:12, p. 4
3:13, pp. 36, 85, 134, 139, 183
3:13–14, p. 135
3:14, p. 134
3:15–18, p. 135
3:16, p. 135
3:19, pp. 69, 70, 71, 75, 77, 80, 120
3:21, p. 126
3:23 – 4:3, p. 129
3:23, p. 129
3:23–24, pp. 39, 77
3:23–24, 4:3, p. 118
3:23–25, p. 132
3:24, pp. 34, 45, 77, 120, 129
3:25, pp. 77, 135
4, p. 35
4:1–3, p. 24
4:1–7, 21–31, p. 129
4:2, p. 129
4:3, p. 14
4:4, pp. 36, 82, 118, 183
4:4–5, pp. 15, 84, 129, 161, 183
4:5, p. 129
4:8, p. 128
4:9, p. 128
4:10, pp. 63, 165
4:21, p. 35
4:24, p. 35
5, p. 182
5:1, pp. 132, 139
5:1, 18, p. 200
5:1–4, p. 69
5:3, pp. 31, 135
5:13, p. 145

5:13–14, p. 146
5:14, p. 24
5:14–15, p. 197
5:16, p. 186
5:16–23, p. 1
5:18, p. 130
5:19–20, p. 182
5:19–21, p. 186
5:22, p. 112
5:22–23, pp. 183, 186
5:23, p. 4
5:24, p. 185
6:2, pp. 24, 94, 146

Ephesians
1:6, 12, 14, p. 91
1:10, p. 17
2:11–22, p. 119
2:14, p. 147
2:14–17, p. 120
2:15, pp. 7, 120
3:3, p. 67
3:4–5, p. 34
3:18, p. 140
4:23, p. 140
4:25, p. 66
4:28, p. 66
5, p. 92
5:18, p. 143
5:19, p. 142
5:19–20, p. 92
5:21, p. 64
5:22–24, p. 64
5:28–33, p. 64
6:1–3, pp. 64, 90
6:2, p. 67
6:4, p. 64

6:5–8, p. 64
6:9, p. 64
6:18, p. 93

Philippians
2:6–11, p. 92
2:8, p. 84
2:9, p. 81
3:6, p. 178
4:6, p. 180

Colossians
2:11, pp. 142, 179
2:11–23, p. 142
2:12, p. 142
2:13–15, p. 142
2:14, p. 120
2:16, p. 166
2:16, 17, p. 142
2:16–17, pp. 63, 78, 165
2:17, pp. 85, 166
2:20–23, pp. 141, 143
3:5, p. 67
3:10, p. 140
3:16, p. 92
3:18, p. 64
3:19, p. 64
3:20, p. 64
3:21, p. 64
3:22–25, p. 64

1 Thessalonians
5:12, p. 64

1 Timothy
1:9–10, pp. 43, 97
4:1–5, p. 143

5:17–20, p. 194
6:17, p. 143

Titus
3:3–7, p. 198
3:5, p. 140

Hebrews
1:1, pp. 78, 208
3:8, p. 167
4, p. 170
4:1–11, p. 168
4:1–12, p. 63
4:3, pp. 154, 166
4:3, 5, p. 153
4:4, p. 153
4:6, p. 153
4:7, p. 153
4:8, p. 153
4:9, p. 153
4:10, p. 166
4:11, p. 153
4:14–5:11, p. 121
7:12, pp. 110, 121
7:22, p. 121
7:24, p. 121
8:5, p. 78
8:7–8, p. 110
8:13, pp. 110, 116
9, p. 85
9:9, p. 85
9:11–12, p. 85
9:12–13, p. 85
9:14, p. 86
9:15, p. 86
9:23, p. 85
9:24, p. 86

9:27, p. 190
10:1, pp. 78, 85, 104
10:1–3, p. 116
10:3–4, p. 116
10:5–10, p. 139
10:7, p. 81
10:10, p. 185
10:14, pp. 122, 185
10:16, p. 89
10:17, p. 86
10:18, p. 86
10:25, p. 162
11:1–7, p. 22
11:2, p. 104
11:9, p. 103
11:10, 14–16, p. 103
11:12, p. 103
11:13, p. 103
11:40, p. 104
12:1, p. 145
12:3–4, p. 189
12:10, p. 184
12:14, p. 187
13:15, p. 91
13:17, p. 64

James
1:25, p. 130
2:8, pp. 14, 24
2:10, pp. 31, 79
2:10–11, pp. 128, 186
2:14–26, p. 127
3:1–2, p. 78
4:1, p. 43
5:13, p. 91

1 Peter

1:7, p. 25
1:15–16, p. 43
1:17, p. 140
2:13–15, p. 64
2:13–17, pp. 93, 148
2:18–25, pp. 64, 93
2:22, p. 118
2:23–25, p. 65
2:24, p. 138
3:1–8, p. 64
3:7, p. 64
3:18, p. 138
4:11, p. 91
5:7, p. 180

2 Peter
1:3–4, p. 187
1:5–7, p. 187
3:18, p. 186

1 John
3:2, p. 189
3:4, pp. 20, 39, 70
3:5–6, 17–18, p. 131
3:22, p. 205
4:16, p. 63
5:2–3, p. 205
5:21, p. 63

Revelation
1, p. 152
1:10, pp. 150, 165
2:6, p. 136
2:14–15, p. 136
6:14, p. 121
7:9, p. 103
17–18, p. 65

Index of Authors

Alderson, Richard 137

Athanasius..........................151

Augustine 169

Bauckham, R.J 1

Bennett, Christopher.........191

Bounds, Nicholas...............171

Buchanan, James................199

Calvin, John13, 28, 75, 77, 87, 136, 143, 170, 179

Carson, D.A. 1

Chrysostom 123, 151

Coates, Gerald....................137

Collinson, Patrick 170

de Lacey, D.R. 1

Fairbairn, A.M........................1

Flavel, John.......................87, 1

Hamelton, Patrick 113

Helm, Paul............................21

Hooker, Richard 171

Ignatius 151

Kendall, R.T.......................137

Kevan, E.F...............3, 1, 125, 1

Klein, M.G. 55

Lewis, C.S. 180

Lincoln, A.T........................155

Luther, Martin....................170

M'Cheyne, Robert Murry.162

Manton, Thomas....................1

Murray, John 1

Owen, John............4, 171, 186

Reisinger, John...................153

Tyndale, William 1

van Gemeren, William........13

Van Gemeren, William 23

Westminster Confession of Faith13, 21, 29, 30, 48, 54, 1, 111, 171, 179

Weymouth............................99

Wilson, Daniel 171

Bibliography

Bauckham, R.J. "Sabbath and Sunday in the Post-Apostolic Church" in *From Sabbath to Lord's Day*, Grand Rapids, Michigan, Zondervan, 1982.

Bennett, Christopher. "The Use of the Mosaic Law in the New Testament Church" in *The End of the Law*. Affinity Conference Paper, Bridgend, Affinity, 2009.

Buchanan, James. *The Office and Work of the Holy Spirit*, Edinburgh/John Johnstone, 1844.

Calvin, John. *Institutes of the Christian Religion*. Ed. J.T. McNeil, Philadelphia, Westminster Press, 1977.

Carson, D.A. *From Sabbath to Lord's Day*, Grand Rapids, Michigan, Zondervan, 1982.

---------------- *Sermon on the Mount*, Carlisle, UK, Paternoster, 1978.

Collinson, Patrick. *Essays in Protestant and Puritan*. London (Publisher not known), 1983.

Fairbairn, A.M. *Revelation of the Law in Scripture*, Grand Rapids, Michigan, Zondervan, 1957.

Flavel, John. *Works, Vol.1*. London, Banner of Truth, 1968.

Gundry, Stanley. *Five Views of Law and Gospel*, Grand Rapids, Zondervan, 1999.

Helm, Paul. "The Place of the Mosaic Law in Society Today," in *The End of the Law?*, Affinity Conference Paper, Bridgend, Affinity, 2009.

Horton, Michael. *Covenant and Salvation Union with Christ*, Philadelphia, Westminster, John Knox, 2001.

Kevan, E.F. *The Moral Law*, Jenkintown, Pennsylvania, Sovereign Grace Publishers, 1963.

-------------------*The Grace of Law*, London. Carey Kingsgate Press, 1964.

-------------------*Keep his Commandments*, London, Tyndale Press, 1964.

Lenski, R.C.H. *Interpretation of Matthew's Gospel*, Minneapolis, Minnesota, Augsburg Publishing House, 1943.

Lincoln, A.T. Article in *From Sabbath to Lord's Day*, Grand Rapids, Michigan, Zondervan, 1982.

Long, Gary D. *Biblical Law and Ethics*, New York, Backus Book Publishers, 1981.

Murray, John: *Principles of Conduct*, London, Tyndale Press, 1957.

Owen, John. *Overcoming Sin and Temptation*, Wheaton, Illinois, Crossway Books, 2006.

Reisinger, John G. *Tablets of Stone*, Frederick, MD, New Covenant Media, 2004.

Tyndale, William. *Works*, London, (Publisher not known), 1861.

van Gemeren, W. Article in *From Sabbath to Lord's Day*, Grand Rapids, Michigan, Zondervan, 1982.

-------------------- *The Law is the Perfection of Righteousness in Jesus Christ* in *Five Views of Law and Gospel*, Grand Rapids, Zondervan, 1999.

Wells, Tom and Zaspel, Fred. *New Covenant Theology*, Frederick, MD, New Covenant Media, 2002.

Westminster Confession of Faith, (City not known), Free Presbyterian Church of Scotland, 195.

www.ingramcontent.com/pod-product-compliance
Lightning Source LLC
LaVergne TN
LVHW052019080426
835513LV00018B/2082